Peter John Stoltzman's

Commercial Piano Workbook II

Table of Contents

Play-along Tracks: Go to this link to access all of the play-along tracks for this workbook. You can download them for free.

https://goo.gl/vrn8ZR

Instructional Videos: Go to this link to access all of the instructional videos for this workbook. You can watch them any time on YouTube.

https://goo.gl/VGX5Bg

Cover Art by Thomas Heflin www.thomasheflin.com

Introduction

This workbook is a continuation of the skills and knowledge developed in my Commercial Piano Workbook I. By the end of working through that book, a piano student should have a basic understanding of sight-reading notes in the treble and bass clefs, playing scales in all keys, and performing and composing standard chord progressions using triads and commercial piano techniques, as well as a basic 12-bar blues. Also, if equipped with LogicPro or similar digital audio workstation (DAW) software, a student should have a fundamental skill set working in that software to create and record tracks and bounce audio files.

Harmony = Flavor

I love the analogy of food to harmony. And harmony is the primary focus of these workbooks. It is the primary function of what a commercial pianist does. Technique, of course, is indispensable...but technique is more like the plates and silverware that serve up and present the food, and the food is the harmony. The flavor (and texture, of course) is what really gives you the emotional experience. And for my money, that equates to the harmony, aka the chords.

In this workbook, students will discover new chord types (sus, add, 7th chords, etc.) and progressions (non-diatonic, ii-V's, etc.). Workbook I basically taught you to make eggs and toast, maybe spaghetti dinner too. You can scramble or fry your eggs, put different sauces on your pasta...but it's all simple. It's solid foundational music: the Four Chord Song progressions and variations, triads and inversions and basic comping techniques. The information in this book is going to greatly expand your harmonic pantry. I think it's useful, actually, to really embrace this food analogy. I'm going to put a bunch of new spices in your spice rack, and show you some tried and true recipes. Then it's going to be up to you to experiment, apply these new flavors creatively, and develop a next level style of cooking up tasty music.

My Goals

These lessons are intended to help you:

    1) Play the piano like contemporary pianists really play.

    2) Understand the skills and concepts involved in your repertoire.

    3) Apply skills and concepts independently.

Assumptions and Pre-requisites

This book is presented with the assumption that the reader is actively studying music. It can be used by an independent learner, but almost certainly will be more effective in conjunction with a class and/or a private instructor. If you do not have a teacher to work with, I strongly recommend accessing the instructional videos on YouTube as you work through each section.

Because each section has notated music examples, it is important for you to have a basic knowledge of music theory. You should have completed my Commercial Piano Workbook I, or have the skill set to execute the Final Test from Workbook I. The most important pre-requisite is a regular commitment to practicing and completing the assignments, in order to progress consistently. The "assignments" in the book are intended to be completed and assessed by a teacher, whereas the "practices" are intended to be worked on at home by students. Depending on the age and ambition of a student, practices may be worked on to varying degrees of thoroughness and mastery.

Technology

I believe that technology has become inextricably linked with music production in the 21st century. You don't have to know technology to know the piano. But if you have professional aspirations in the industry as a performer, songwriter, or producer, developing relevant technology skills will make you more viable and valuable in many scenarios. This book is full of opportunities to utilize LogicPro software to record with play-along tracks, and to create demo recordings of original compositions. If you don't own or have access to LogicPro, I highly recommend purchasing the $200 program from Apple. That price is incredibly low considering the scope of the software. You'll need a Mac for that, though.

Using LogicPro, I have created demos to prep bands for concerts, recorded on other artists' albums, and mixed my own trio album, as well as creating dozens of play-along tracks for my piano classes. I also use LogicPro in conjunction with the performance software, Mainstage, which enables me to program sound combinations for entire sets using midi controller keyboards. It sure beats lugging a Rhodes, Minimoog, Wurly, and organ around (unless you have a road team doing that for you!).

Ultimately, you can learn the piano skills in this book without the technology piece, but LogicPro will make it more fun, and give you the beginning of a serious and flexible professional skill set. Many other digital audio workstation (DAW) software setups will provide what you need to complete the technology assignments in this book as well. You just need to be able to import mp3 files, create and record MIDI instrumental tracks, and export audio files when projects are complete.

Teachers

If you're a teacher using this book, I have organized it with section reviews that help you to organize your syllabus or lesson plans. If you don't do LogicPro assignments, you can still have students play those assignments live with largely the same result. You and your students can access all the play-along tracks online.

The instructional videos can be helpful in numerous ways—for students who need reiteration of techniques, for teachers who assign independent practice prior to classes/lessons, and for teachers to see how I demonstrate lessons and perform examples. Accommodate different levels of proclivity and ambition by having students learn one exercise/jam from a section, or all of them. Have advanced students transpose more. Remember, an 8 year-old completing this workbook may look very different than a college music student.

I sincerely hope that you sincerely enjoy working through this book!

About the Author

Peter John Stoltzman is a pianist and educator, who has been the Piano Area Head in CU Denver's Music & Entertainment Industry Studies Department, the Faculty Director and Co-Director of the Mentor Fellowship Program at the Stanford Jazz Workshop, and he is the co-founder and Co-Academic Director of the LYNX Music Industry Program for high school students.

Peter has a bachelor's degree in Jazz Performance from Berklee College of Music, a master's degree in Jazz Composition with a Concentration in Music in Education from New England Conservatory, and a doctoral degree in Music and Human Learning from the University of Texas at Austin. He has been a teacher, performer, composer, arranger, songwriter, producer, and mix engineer.

After Berklee, Peter lived in New York City, where he made Hip Hop tracks for Warner Brothers, and recorded and performed with an eclectic variety of artists including Cuban saxophonist/composer Yosvanny Terry, drummer Deantoni Parks and Kudu, guitarist John Shannon and Waking Vision, American Music Award-winning funk band The Bomb Squad, and singer Javier Colon. In 2010, Peter won first prize in the Phillips Jazz Piano Competition.

Peter has performed around the globe with his father, Grammy-winning clarinetist, Richard Stoltzman, including Carnegie Hall and the Hollywood Bowl. He has toured and recorded with drummer Steve Gadd, bassist Eddie Gomez, and marimbist Mika Yoshida, in Japan and the U.S. He has two releases on Blue Canoe Records - with the jazz quintet, The New Five (2009), and the Ron Westray/Thomas Heflin project (2010). Peter has independently released a 3-CD package of all original music (a finalist for the 2005 Independent Music Awards), a solo piano CD, and the trio CD, "Walk the Path." Peter's second trio CD, "Live at Casa Karen," was released on Bus Biscuit Records in 2013. From 2016-2018, he has recorded albums with Coexistence Trio, The Democracy (jazz quintet), drummer Wayne Salzmann, singer-songwriter Owen Kortz, Brazilian guitarist Gabriel Santiago, saxophonist Mark Fox, and his own New Standards Project (feat. Natalie Cressman and Allison Miller).

www.peterjohnstoltzman.com

The language of musical harmony is an absolutely extra-ordinary one: it's a way of navigating one's emotional frameworks, but without the need to put things into words.

And I think that, as with many other languages, it doesn't matter how many words you can say, how many phrases you know. What matters is the emotional choices you make with this language.

So I encourage us to embrace this idea as a community...which in time may grow us towards, as opposed to away from, our own humanity.

- Jacob Collier

Behaviors of a Successful Contemporary Keyboard Player

If you want to learn a complex skill, one of the best things you can do is to articulate what you're trying to do in statements that begin with verbs. Verbs are action words, and they express with at least some precision what exactly you intend to do. Learning cannot be just thoughts in your head. Learning has to become your behavior. Think about that. Your behavior demonstrates your learning.

Below is my list of the behaviors of a successful contemporary keyboard player. Take a few minutes to read it, and consider each of these verb statements—are these things that you already do? Where are the challenges for you? I hope that you will come back to this list when you complete this workbook, and take stock of your own tangible growth as a contemporary keyboard player.

1) Engage in the Learning Process
- Show up consistently and punctually
- Listen actively and maintain focus
- Seek help when needed
- Offer help when able
- Practice consistently
- Practice to the point of internalizing knowledge, skills, and repertoire
- Independently apply skills
- Transfer skills to various contexts

2) Perform Repertoire
- Play standard song forms and excerpts or phrases
- Recognize standard and non-standard forms and progressions
- Apply appropriate comping techniques
- Adjust technique and thinking spontaneously and/or with practice
- Count off and play at an appropriate tempo
- Keep time and form with or without accompaniment
- Recover from mistakes without stopping or starting over
- Play with appropriate dynamics
- Play with appropriate articulation
- Play with stylistically appropriate "feel"

3) Understand and Utilize Contemporary Chord Theory
- Read chord symbols and form appropriate chord voicings
- Utilize inversions to minimize hand movement and/or voice melodies
- Transpose chords and progressions using numerical analysis

Self-Assessment

     Now that you've given this list some thought, I want you to actually give yourself a numbered rating for each behavior. (1 = lowest, 10 = highest)

- Show up consistently and punctually

    1   2   3   4   5   6   7   8   9   10

- Listen actively and maintain focus

1   2   3   4   5   6   7   8   9   10

- Seek help when needed

    1   2   3   4   5   6   7   8   9   10

- Offer help when able

    1   2   3   4   5   6   7   8   9   10

- Practice consistently

    1   2   3   4   5   6   7   8   9   10

- Practice to the point of internalizing knowledge, skills, and repertoire

    1   2   3   4   5   6   7   8   9   10

- Independently apply skills

    1   2   3   4   5   6   7   8   9   10

- Transfer skills to various contexts

    1   2   3   4   5   6   7   8   9   10

- Play standard song forms and excerpts or phrases

    1   2   3   4   5   6   7   8   9   10

- Recognize standard and non-standard forms and progressions

    1   2   3   4   5   6   7   8   9   10

- Apply appropriate comping techniques

    1   2   3   4   5   6   7   8   9   10

- Adjust technique and thinking spontaneously and/or with practice

    1   2   3   4   5   6   7   8   9   10

- Count off and play at an appropriate tempo

    1   2   3   4   5   6   7   8   9   10

- Keep time and form with or without accompaniment

    1   2   3   4   5   6   7   8   9   10

- Recover from mistakes without stopping or starting over

    1   2   3   4   5   6   7   8   9   10

- Play with appropriate dynamics

    1   2   3   4   5   6   7   8   9   10

- Play with appropriate articulation

    1   2   3   4   5   6   7   8   9   10

- Play with stylistically appropriate "feel"

    1   2   3   4   5   6   7   8   9   10

- Read chord symbols and form appropriate chord voicings

    1   2   3   4   5   6   7   8   9   10

- Utilize inversions to minimize hand movement and/or voice melodies

    1   2   3   4   5   6   7   8   9   10

- Transpose chords and progressions using numerical analysis

    1   2   3   4   5   6   7   8   9   10

Content Review

In the first workbook, you developed foundational knowledge and skills regarding piano geography, intervals, chords voicings, progressions, and comping techniques.

To review, read and play everything through page 10. The more keys you can transpose this into, the more you are on your way to mastering contemporary piano skills. (Remember, "transpose" means to play the same technique and/or progressions in a different key.)

Chord Symbols

For every chord, there is a chord symbol.

A chord symbol provides you with all the basic information you need to construct a chord–the chord type, the root of the chord and the bass note.

What the chord symbol doesn't do is tell you anything about the musical style, or what techniques to use to perform that chord. The figure above shows the notes of a C major triad and the LH bass notes on the grand staff, but contemporary lead sheets may only show a chord symbol, over lyrics, or with slashes in the bars, like this:

The chord symbol, C, can be read as "C," or as "C major."

If you are given a lead sheet (aka a "chart") you can play chords in any number of ways. Chord symbols give the performer interpretive freedom. But of course, you must still make your choices as to what to play within the constraints of the style.

NOTE: Your left hand (LH) should default to playing single notes (or grabbing octaves) in the low range of the piano, while your right hand (RH) defaults to playing chords in the middle and upper range of the piano.

Inversions of a Triad

There are three notes in a major triad, and therefore three possible inversions.

Shape Groups on the Piano

Playing in all 12 keys can be daunting. Dividing the keys by the physical shapes on the piano helps create shortcuts by grouping chord shapes in your brain and in your fingers.

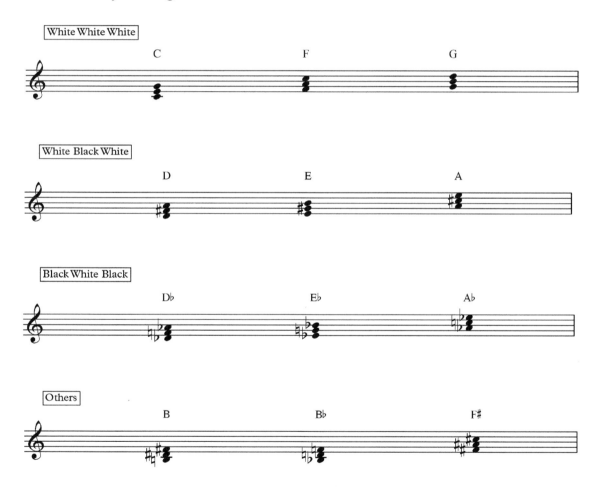

Assignment

Practice playing each major triad in all three inversions.

In the Key

Being "in the key of" C (or any other key) means a few things:

1) There is an established harmonic "home," or tonic, which is numbered in analysis as the Arabic numeral 1, or the Roman numeral **I**.

2) There is a scale that correlates to the key. Notes that are in the scale are called diatonic. Notes that are not in the scale are non-diatonic. Single notes are numbered in analysis with Arabic numerals–1 through 7.

3) Each note in the scale correlates to a chord as well. These chords are called diatonic chords, and are numbered in analysis with Roman numerals–**I** through **vii**. The Roman numerals are capitalized for major chords and lower case for minor chords.

The diatonic chords in the key of C are:

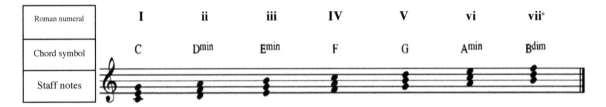

Assignment

After successfully completing Workbook I, you should be able to play major scales in all 12 keys. Review your scales, paying attention to the numerical analysis of the notes in each key. Notice that C is the 1 in the key of C, the 2 in the key of B♭, the 3 in the key of A♭, and so on.

After reviewing major scales, play through at least one key from each "shape group" with diatonic triads in your RH and single notes in your LH. Name each chord symbol and its Roman numeral in the key. Notice the shifting relationships. For instance, a C major triad is the **I** in the key of C, but the **V** in the key of F, and the **IV** in the key of G.

Practice: Transpose and Invert

If you really want a next level challenge, transpose the diatonic triads in all keys and play them in 1st inversion and 2nd inversion shapes!

Minor Chords

The "minor third" = "the flat 3."
So a C minor chord has E♭ in the middle.

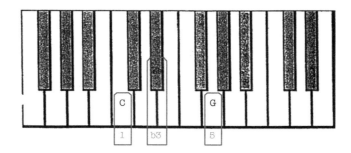

Your C minor chord symbol should look like this:

Practice: Transpose

Play both major *and minor* triads in 12 keys.

Relative Minor

The key of A minor actually has exactly the same notes and chords as C major—but the tonic is different. With A as the tonic, or i chord, C is no longer **I**. In the key of A minor, C is the **♭III**. *Chord symbols are universal, and analysis is relative.*

The visual below shows the key of C major overlapping with the key of A minor.

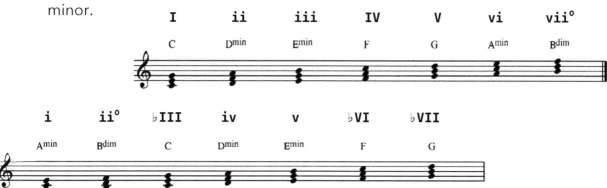

Practice: Transpose

Name the relative minor key of each major key. For example, D minor is the relative minor of F major. Play the major triad and then the relative minor triad.

Section Review

Skills
Play major and minor triads in 12 keys.
Play major and minor triads in 1st and 2nd inversion.

Terminology
Triad
Chord symbol
Inversions
Diatonic ("in the key")
Major
Minor
Relative minor

Assignments
Practice playing each major triad in all three inversions.
Play major scales in 12 keys.
Play diatonic triads in multiple keys.

Repertoire Review

Workbook I began with jamming on single notes, and culminated in the 12 bar blues, and in the modern four-chord progressions that are found in the majority of popular music today. The following examples focus on the techniques and chord progressions from the second half of the book.

Progressions Using Major and Minor Chords

Pop/Rock Jam in F

Hip Hop Jam in C

Rock Ballad Jam in E♭

Assignment

Analyze the above progressions with Roman numerals by writing in the Roman numerals next to the chord symbols. Choose at least one jam to perform live with the play-along track(s).

"Four Chord Song" Progressions

1. Key: G

| I | V | vi | IV |

2. Key: D

| IV | I | V | vi |

3. Key: F

| vi | IV | I | V |

Assignment

Write out the chord symbols above the Roman numerals, and play these progressions with the play-along tracks.

The 12 Bar Blues

Below is the boogie-woogie style blues that you learned at the end of Workbook I.

Assignment

Perform this blues with the play-along track.

Write in the chord symbols above the staff.

Jam

Improvise over the blues! You can either improvise in a piano duet with your teacher or a fellow student, or jam with the play-along track.

Section Review

Skills
Play short songs with major and minor triads, varying techniques, and in varying keys.
Play a boogie-woogie 12 bar blues.

Terminology
"Four Chord Song"
12 bar blues

Assignments
Analyze chord progressions with Roman numerals.
Write in chord symbols above the staff.
Perform live with play-along track(s).

Expanding Your Technique

A More Pianistic Technique

In Workbook I, most of the focus was on RH techniques—chunking, double-time chunking, broken chords, and arpeggios. Almost every example had some variation on one of those RH techniques, and a simple bass line in the LH. Now, it's time to expand what your LH can do.

Think of your LH as the bass player in a band. Sometimes a simple part is all that is needed, but sometimes a bass player can get bored with just playing the roots of chords. The following exercises and jams will give your LH some new techniques to work with. With practice, you will begin to play in a more "pianistic" way, with a technique that sounds like you really know how to play this instrument.

LH Technique Variations

These techniques, using other chord tones thank just the 1, will create harmonic *and rhythmic* tension and release in your LH. You will hear these types of LH techniques used in folk, country, R&B, pop, latin, jazz, Broadway, and all styles of singer/songwriter music. Listen to the LH of artists such as John Legend or Sarah McLachlan, or classic piano driven songs like Steely Dan's "Sail the Waterway," or more current songs like Bruno Mars' "When I Was Your Man." You will hear that the rhythm of the piano part has additional rhythmic propulsion, and that is because of the interplay between RH and LH techniques.

1 - 5 variations

Sometimes referred to as "alternating bass," the 1 and 5 can be used over any chord. Listen to some Bluegrass, and you'll hear the bass doing it all the time.

1) Country/Folk Rock Jam

2) Pop Ballad Jam

1 - 5 - 8 variations

Adding the octave into the 1-5 bass opens up even more rhythmic possibilities. You'll hear pianists use the 1-5-8 shape a lot in their LH, because it just fits so perfectly into an adult hand on the piano, creating movement in a piano part in virtually any style.

1) R&B Ballad Jam

2) 70s Shuffle Jam (swung 1/8th notes)

1 - 3 - 5 variations

A triad can also be an effective LH part. Many songs with a Latin feel use triadic bass lines, for example Ritchie Valens' classic hit, "La Bamba." But triad techniques such as the classical Alberti bass technique have also been used to create hit pop songs, for example The Fray's "How to Save a Life."

1) Arpeggio Jam

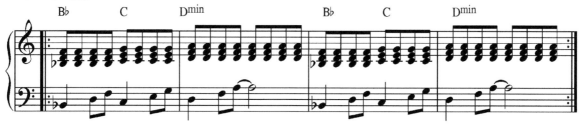

2) Alberti Bass Jam

3) Triplet Arpeggio Jam

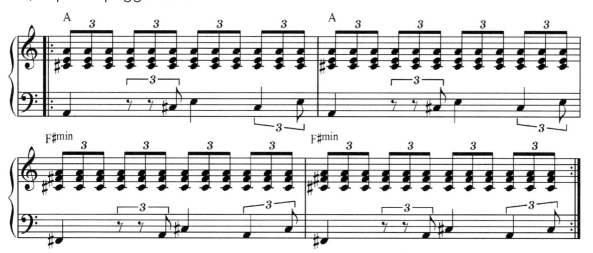

Ba Doom technique

The LH can also utilize the 5 or the octave as a quick "pickup note." This gives an almost casual, intuitive sounding movement to the LH. In fact, most pianists use this type of technique intuitively, to create that "ba doom" effect.

1) Pop Ballad Jam

2) Funky Reggae Jam

Assignment

Perform at least one of the Jams from pp. 12-15 with a play-along track.

RH Technique Variations

I'm not trying to leave the RH out entirely, of course! I want you to get a feel for some RH variations that are actually *simpler* and some that are more complex than what you are used to.

RH Static Shapes

Almost all of the chord-based knowledge and skill you have developed to this point has been in the context of moving the RH chords and the LH bass notes to create chord progressions. However, one of the often overlooked and undervalued RH technique variations used by modern pianists in commercial music is the RH static shape. In other words, the RH maintains a chord or pattern, while the LH moves underneath. This can create an implied chord progression, while also keeping a certain continuous harmonic/melodic/rhythmic texture on top, and the result can be very satisfying to the ear.

The Power Chord

Pop/Rock music has had a long and happy relationship with power chords—from Marc Cohn's "Walkin' in Memphis" to hundreds of heavy metal songs, to almost every U2 hit, to John Legend's "All of You."

Power chords are played by removing the 3 from a triad. This gives you just the 1 and the 5, which is a very strong sound. The power chord can be played with an octave added, or just with the 1 and 5, and you can use any of the standard comping techniques you already know—chunking, double-time chunking, arpeggios, broken chords.

1) Chunking Power Chords Jam in C

2) Syncopated Chunking Jam in A

3) Adding the Octave Jam in E ♭

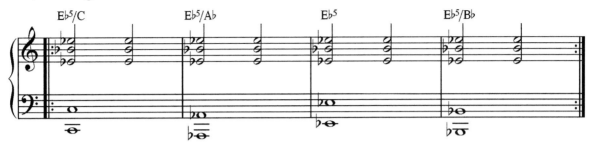

4) Broken Power Chords Jam in D

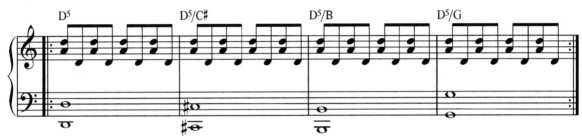

Major Triad - the I chord

Pianists also sometimes just use the **I** chord as a static pattern in the RH. This creates a certain amount of tension and repetition that can be a little grating after a while, but it can be an effective technique if used tastefully.

1) Arpeggio Jam in B

2) Broken Chord Jam in A ♭

3) Double-time Chunking Jam in D ♭

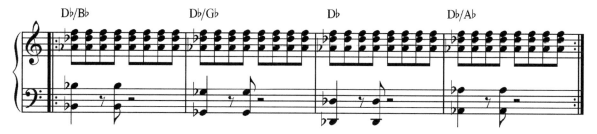

Practice: Transpose

Play power chords in all 12 keys.

Assignment

Perform at least one of the Jams from pp. 16-18 with a play-along track.

LogicPro Application

Record a piano part with one or more of the play-along tracks.

Voicing the Melody

In Workbook I, you worked on chord inversions. And I explained that there are two reasons to use inversions: 1) to create easy physical movement between chords, which also produces nice "voice leading," and 2) to "voice the melody" of a song. Now's your chance to explore what it means to voice the melody.

Essentially, all that means is that the top note of your chord matches the melody. Dig a little deeper and you realize that "the melody" could actually be a vocal or instrumental melody, or it could just be a melodic figure that you want the piano part to emphasize. Try to play the following examples, and recognize how the top note of your RH chords creates a melodic line.

1) Soul Jam

2) 80s TV Show Theme Jam

3) Pop R&B Jam

4) Rock Songwriter Jam

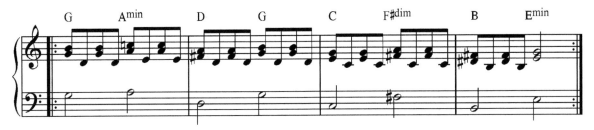

Assignment

Perform at least one of the Jams from pp. 18-19 with a play-along track.

Pro Tips from Dr. Peter

Thinking Ahead

One common challenge that students face when learning the piano is transitioning from chord to chord, section to section, without hesitation. You can't really enjoy performing if you're hesitating, and a listener won't enjoy it either... But playing in a perfect rhythmic flow is easier said than done!

You have to train your brain to think ahead. This is absolutely crucial to performing. As you practice, get each little part (a chord, a bar, four bars, whatever you can master easily) to the point where you can relax and enjoy watching your fingers play. Then, as you're playing one little part, you need to think ahead to the next little part—anticipate where your fingers will go. Get it? Try it!

I want you to practice this now, if possible. If you feel overwhelmed learning something new, just use something you've already learned. For instance, example number 4 on page 19. In this example, the chords change every two beats.

Follow these steps to practice thinking ahead:

1) Separate the example into two-beat parts (e.g., the G broken chords, then the Amin broken chords, then the D, etc.), and practice each one alone until it is easy for you. This first step is crucial. There's no use in thinking ahead if your fingers don't know where to go.

2) Then, practice playing the first two beats and thinking ahead. Stop on the last note before transitioning to the new chord. Are your fingers ready to move? Can you see and/or feel on the piano where your new destination is?

3) Practice again, thinking ahead, and this time go to the new chord and stop! If you can't do it, you need to slow the tempo down. You are actually writing a pattern in your brain—the pattern of thinking ahead!

4) Repeat step 3 as many times as needed, speeding up the tempo after you can nail the transition, until you reach the desired tempo and can consciously think ahead and play through it with ease.

5) Continue adding the two-beat parts, practicing in this manner. Each time you add a new part, it becomes a new challenge for your brain to be able to transition, execute, and think ahead.

Remember to slow things down, and focus on writing that "thinking ahead program" in your brain. Then as you speed up, it will be there in your process. Eventually, thinking ahead only takes a millisecond. It becomes a hardened habit in your brain.

Section Review

Skills

Play LH techniques using the 1, 5, and 8, or arpeggio patterns of the triad.
Play RH techniques using power chords and triads as static shapes over moving bass lines.
Transpose power chords.
Play short examples using triad inversions to voice a melody.

Terminology

"Alternating bass"
Voicing the melody

Assignments

Perform at least one of the LH Variation Jams.
Perform at least one of the RH Variation Jams.
Use LogicPro to record with a play-along track.

More Shapes and Sounds

There are so many great variations on standard chords–different chord types, different chord progressions, different chord voicings. Let's go over some other chord types now. If you've mastered major and minor chords, you've probably been exposed to some of the chords below. If this is your first time studying chords, brace yourself. Either way, this section contains potent information that will supply you with a professional-level arsenal of possibilities at your fingertips. It will take years of practice and experience to retain and master all of this, though. So be as patient and as diligent as you can.

New Chord Types: sus 4 and sus 2

"Sus" chords are characterized by a *suspension* of their harmonic quality–minor or major. Pop quiz: Which note gives a chord a minor or major quality? Answer: "The 3"

If you're still not sure you get that:
Sing the notes of a major triad in root position–1, 3, 5...
Now sing the notes of a minor triad in root position–1, ♭ 3, 5...
That's a huge difference that the 3 (or ♭ 3) makes!

If you move the 3 up to the 4, or down to the 2, you *suspend the harmonic quality* of the chord–you make it a sus chord. Oftentimes suspensions are "resolved," as in the sus 4 resolving to the major 3. But other times they are left hanging, or used as an alternative to the typical chord in any given situation.

Try these voicings in your RH, while playing the root with your LH. Apply a little creativity and you can create an almost infinite array of music with these voicings alone.

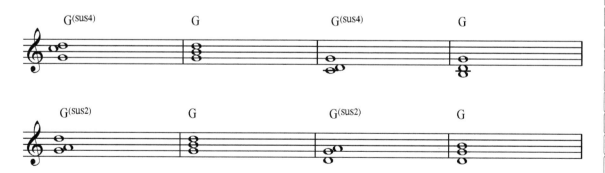

Practice: Transpose

Transpose these chord voicings to all keys.

Sus Chord Jams

1) sus4 Chunking Jam

2) sus4 Syncopated Rock Jam

3) sus2 Pop/Rock Jam

4) sus4 Static Shape Jam

Assignment

Perform at least one of the sus chord jams with a play-along track.

New Chord Types: add 4 and add 2

"Add" chords are similar to sus chords, except they are not suspending the quality at all. They are enhancing (hopefully) the quality, by adding the 2 or the 4 into the mix. There are many ways that you can voice these chords. Here are just a few examples.

Practice: Transpose

Transpose these chord voicings to all keys.

Add Chord Jams

1) Minor add2 Hip Hop Jam

2) Major add2 Ballad Jam

3) Major add4 Static Shape Jam

Assignment

Perform at least one of the add chord jams with a play-along track.

New Chord Types: Diminished and Augmented

If you've taken a traditional harmony or music theory class, you've already studied diminished and augmented triads. The truth is, they're not used that often nowadays. But they definitely have their moments! If you haven't used a diminished or augmented chord effectively, you're missing out. There is a great example of both a diminished 7th chord and augmented 7th chord in R. Kelly's "I Believe I Can Fly." Both chord types create tension—and give an extra twinge of tension compared to a plain old **V–I** progression.

You can remember these chords by simply associating the meaning of their names with their root position shape. Diminished is smaller, augmented is larger.

NOTE: The chord symbol for diminished can be dim, or it can be $^{\circ}$, as in G$^{\circ}$.
The chord symbol for augmented can be aug, or it can be $^{+}$, as in G^{+}.

Practice: Transpose

Transpose diminished and augmented triads to all keys.

Diminished Chord Jams

1) Dim. Pop Chunking Jam

2) **i** dim Gospel Broken Chord Jam

Augmented Jam

1) **I** aug Pop/Rock Jam

2) **V** aug Rock/R&B Arpeggio Jam

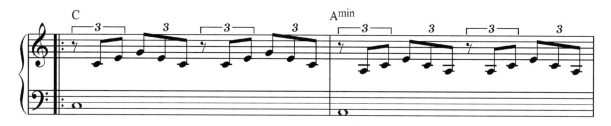

Assignment

Perform at least one of the above jams with a play-along track.

LogicPro Application

Record a piano part with one or more of the play-along tracks in this section.

Section Review

Skills

Play and transpose sus chords and add chords.

Play and transpose diminished and augmented chords.

Terminology

Sus 2, sus 4

Add 2, add 4

Diminished

Augmented

Assignments

Perform an add chord jam live with play-along track(s).

Perform a sus chord jam live with play-along track(s).

Perform a diminished or augmented chord jam live with play-along track(s).

Record with a play-along track using LogicPro.

Leading Chords

Leading Diminished Chords

In Workbook I, you learned that diatonic diminished chords are rarely, if ever, used in commercial music. However, diminished chords do show up from time to time, creating tension in chord progressions. That tension can be like the perfect squeeze of lemon on a grilled salmon fillet (yes!), or it can be like grapefruit after brushing your teeth (no!!). There are a few places where diminished chords are commonly used, but at this point I want you to just focus on one: leading to minor chords from a half step below.

Practice: Transpose

Choose a minor key and play the diminished leading chord and resolve it up to the minor triad. Check off the box next to the key, and try to get all 12!

□ A	□ G
□ B	□ Db/C#
□ C	□ Eb/D#
□ D	□ Gb/F#
□ E	□ Ab/G#
□ F	□ Bb/A#

Leading Diminished Chord Jams

Play through these jams to get a taste of the flavor of the diminished chord approaching a minor chord from a half step below in context.

1) **vii°** to **i** Jam

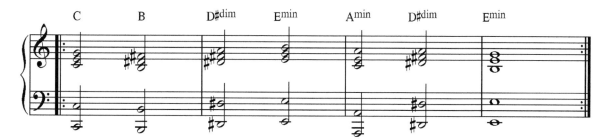

2) **#ii°** to **iii** Jam

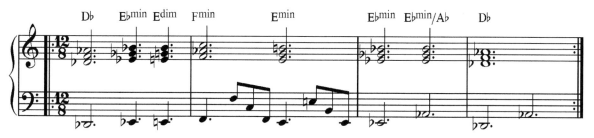

28

3) **♯v°** to **vi** Jam

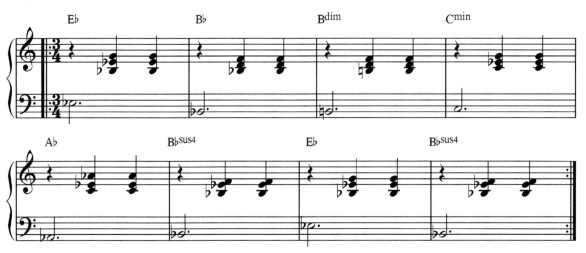

Assignment

Perform at least one of the above jams with a play-along track.

Leading Tone Slash Chords

Leading tone slash chords are really, really important. Don't skip this.

Do you know what the leading tone is?

It's the note one half step below the root. In solfege, that's "ti," and it leads to "do." In numbers, it's 7, and it leads to 8 (or 1).

For example, in the key of C, the leading tone is B. In the key of D, the leading tone is C#.

Ok, so you know what the leading tone is.

Now, I want you to take a look at the leading tone slash chord below–play it, and try to understand it before I explain it.

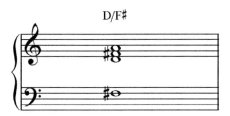

Question: What note is the leading tone? And where is it leading?

Answer: The leading tone is F♯, and it's leading to G.

So here's the deal with the leading tone slash chord: It's just a **V** chord over its own third (instead of its root). At the end of Workbook I, I introduced you to this chord as a substitution for the **vii°**. Now you can expand your concept of this special kind of slash chord.

D is the **V** in the key of G, the third of D is F♯, and F♯ is the leading tone of G. Hence, the D/F♯ chord–the leading tone slash chord. These chords are all over popular music today. A great example is Sarah Bareilles's "Love Song." Or you can go back to classic piano rock songs like Paul McCartney's "Maybe I'm Amazed."

Traditional harmony has analyses of the leading tone slash chord, based on the inversion and function, but that misses out on the chord's transferability. The coolest thing about leading tone slash chords is that you can use them anywhere. They sound great even when they're not leading anywhere. And also, you can use them to lead to wherever you want to go. If you want to lead to G, a great option is D/F♯. If you want to lead to C, use G/B.

Practice: Transpose

Choose a major key and play the leading tone slash chord and resolve it up to the major triad. Check off the box next to the key, and try to get all 12!

□ A	□ G
□ B	□ D♭/C♯
□ C	□ E♭/D♯
□ D	□ G♭/F♯
□ E	□ A♭/G♯
□ F	□ B♭/A♯

PRO TIPS FROM DR. PETER

The Chord Progression is The Journey

These leading chords create the anticipation of arrival. The feeling of anticipation is the key! It's the emotional mechanism that hooks a listener's attention, and makes their experience less predictable. Psychology research has shown that anticipation is one of the most potent mental experiences. Think about movie scores, and how powerfully the music can correlate with the anticipation of a significant moment, be it awe-inspiring, terrifying, or tear-jerking. Audiences want to be moved, and for that, they need to be led on a journey toward a satisfying destination. Regardless of whether the destination is expected or unexpected, it is the feeling of anticipation that captures the audience's imagination.

So if you feel like your composition or your piano part needs more depth, try inserting a leading chord into your progression. I think you'll be excited by what you discover. Lead to an expected chord. Lead to an unexpected chord. Experiment!

Extra Hip Variation: sus 2 and add 2 Leading tone slash chords

    If you like the leading tone slash chord, try it with a triad variation, rather than just a plain old triad. The best of these is the sus 2 or add 2 chord (played over its third). So much tasty music in these chords…explore, enjoy, and employ these shapes and sounds in your own music.

Leading Tone Slash Chord Jams

1) Descending Diatonic Jam

2) Ascending Diatonic Jam

3) 70s sus2 add2 Jam

4) Cinematic Jam

Assignment

Perform at least one of the above jams with a play-along track.

LogicPro Application

Record a piano part with one or more of the play-along tracks in this section.

Composition

Compose a four bar repeating chord progression.
Above the slashes, write the chord symbols.
• Use appropriate inversions—don't jump from root position to root position.
• Choose a technique and stick with it—chunking, broken chords, arpeggios.
• Play a pattern in 4/4 meter, with a rhythm you can tap your foot to.
• Don't write a key signature, but be conscious of what chord is the tonic.
• Use at least one leading diminished chord *and* one leading tone slash chord.
• Make an intentional choice about whether you resolve your leading chords to expected or unexpected chords. What feeling are you creating?

1)

2)

LogicPro Application

Now is a good opportunity to create a recording independently with LogicPro. Choose one of your four bar compositions and record it on LogicPro.

1) Open LogicPro and start a new Empty Project.

2) Create one "software instrument" track.

3) Assign a piano or electric piano sound to the first track.

4) Create a second software instrument track, and assign a bass sound.

5) Consider what tempo you want your demo to be, and change the tempo marking as needed.

6) Use the Drummer tool in LogicPro X, or find a drum loop to use for your demo, by searching through the Loops. (Or, if you know how to create your own drum track, go for it.)

<u>If you want to use a loop:</u>

Open the Loops tab, click on All Drums, and scroll through the thousands of loops. Loops with a blue icon are audio files; loops with a green icon are MIDI files. The drum loops will play at the tempo marking you have set for your track. Audio tracks recorded at a different tempo will sound strange, but MIDI tracks will translate to any tempo.

Once you find a drum loop that will work for your demo, drag it into an empty space underneath your keyboard and bass tracks. It should create its own track.

7) Record your bass part and keyboard part in any order. Use the editing tools and quantize as you desire.

8) Bounce your track to an mp3 and save it to your USB Key.

Assignment

Play through the exercise below. If you are ambitious, start the progression a half-step higher, on A♭/C, and play through the other 6 keys. To take it to the next level, substitute sus 2 chords in your LT Slash Chords, e.g., G^{sus2}/B.

Leading Tone Slash Chord
Chromatic Exercise

Section Review

Skills

Play diminished triads, and resolve them up a half step to minor triads.
Play leading tone slash chords and resolve them up a half step to major or minor triads.
Perform two-handed piano parts using leading chords, from grand staff notation and chord symbols.

Terminology

Leading diminished chords
Leading tone slash chords

Assignments

Perform a leading diminished chord jam with a play-along track.
Compose at least two 4-bar progressions, using leading chords.
Record your original composition using LogicPro.
Play the leading tone slash chord chromatic exercise.

Non-Diatonic Progressions

There are times when music can get a lot more interesting if the harmony goes outside the box—even just a little! One well-timed minor chord when the ear is expecting major can create involuntary emotional responses. One strategically placed ♭**VI** chord instead of the **I** can inspire comments like, "You're a genius!" Trust me, you don't have to be a genius…these are tricks that film score composers use all the time, and most good songwriters use whether they understand the theory behind it or not.

Modal Borrowing

One primary way to create nice non-diatonic progressions is to borrow chords from another diatonic realm—e.g., if you're in the key of C major, you can borrow chords from the key of C minor. As you learn more theory, you can delve deeper into modal borrowing and use scales such as phrygian and lydian, etc.

Diatonic triads in C major

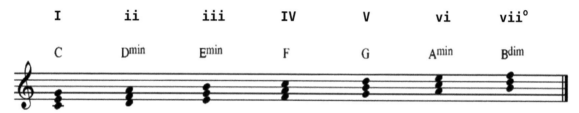

Diatonic triads in C minor

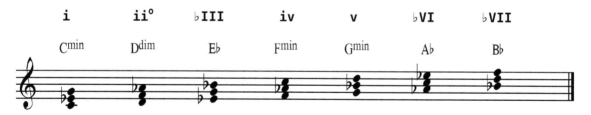

Practice: Major key, borrowing from Minor key

    1) **I** - **vi** versus **I** - ♭**VI**
Play a C major triad, then an Amin triad. Play C major, then Ab major.
    2) **I** - **iv** versus **I** - **iv**
Play C major, then F major. Play C major, then Fmin.
    3) **I** - **iii** versus **I** - ♭**III**
Play C major, then Emin. Play C major, then Eb major.

Practice: Minor key, borrowing from Major key

1) **i** - **v** versus **i** - **V**
Play a C minor triad, then a Gmin triad. Play C minor, then G major.
2) **i** - **iv** versus **i** - **IV**
Play C minor, then F minor. Play C minor, then F major.
3) **i** - ♭**VII** versus **i** - **vii**°
Play C minor, then Bb major. Play C minor, then B diminished.

Practice: Transpose

Transpose the above practice examples to other keys and play on cue.

Assignment

Write out the major and minor key diatonic chords in F—note names and chord symbols.

I   ii   iii   IV   V   vi   vii°

i   ii°   ♭III   iv   v   ♭VI   ♭VII

Pro Tips from Dr. Peter

Minor Keys are Weird!

It's easy to get a little hung up on minor key harmony, because there are so many variations on the minor scale—natural minor, melodic minor, harmonic minor, and dorian minor, to name a few. If you're a true harmony nerd (like me), you can spend many hours dissecting the different diatonic chords that are found in each minor variation. However, at this point, I don't recommend that—too much thinking.

What you need to know, and remember forever, is that the essential part of most minor modes is 1-2-b3-4-5. Then, the 6 and 7 are changeable (or interchangeable), depending on the sound you're trying to create. If you're ambitious, I highly recommend that you go through 12 keys, play a minor triad, and play 1-2-b3-4-5-4-b3-2-1 with your RH. Get used to the shape and feeling of that in your fingers, so that when you think of a minor key, you can go straight to the first 5 notes in that key as your "home base."

Then, don't get too hung up on the rest of the variations. They're just different combinations of 6 and 7 (natural or flat). Pay attention to the music you learn and listen to, and you'll discover how those various combinations can be used, how they sound, and how they feel to you.

Temporary Modulation

Another common way to move out of a diatonic realm is to change keys. There are many ways to change keys, including just changing keys! However, for now let's focus on one particular vehicle–the leading tone slash chord.

1)

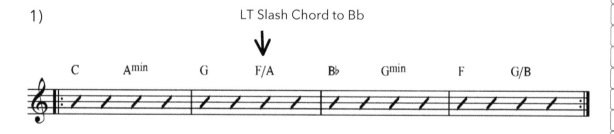

2)

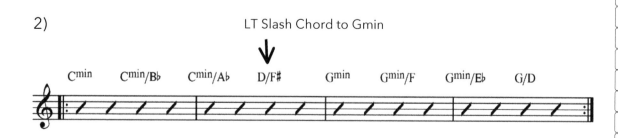

Secondary Dominants

Secondary dominants are chords that function as **V** chords, but resolving somewhere in the key other than the **I**. This can create a temporary feeling of modulation, but more often it just creates an extra layer of tension and release in a chord progression. Think of secondary dominants as "the **V** of..." For example, in the key of C, G is the **V**, and D minor is the **ii** chord. But D *major* is the **V** of G. And if you want an unexpected flavor combination, you might use D major rather than minor. The examples below take you through some of the most common uses of secondary dominants.

1) **III** to the **vi** Jam in Bb

2) **I** to the **IV** Jam in C

3) **VI** to the **ii** Jam in D

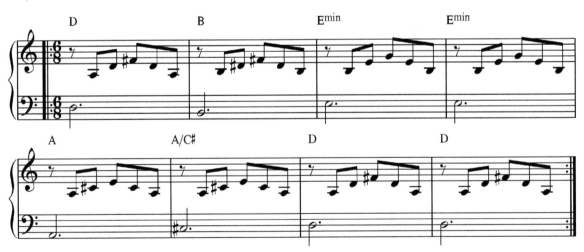

Toolbox

In the non-metaphorical world, you can procure and fill a toolbox in very different ways. For instance, you can go to a big store and purchase a nicely organized, pre-filled toolbox, or you can use whatever materials you have at your disposal to construct your own DIY toolbox, and only fill it with tools you make yourself. Or, perhaps you fall somewhere in between, and you want a little of both—pre-made materials and self-made materials.

Constructing a harmonic progression is much the same. You can use templates that you get directly from other players or from books (such as the templates I'm giving you below). On the other hand, you can create new progressions by experimenting with whatever materials you have. Or, if you're like me, you want a little of both—to know as many templates as you can, and then use your imagination and intuition to create unique sounds.

All of the exercises in this workbook can act as pre-made tools, but they can also act as jumping-off points for you to apply your creative imagination with. Below, I give you a handful of common progressions—you can practice them, transpose them, and perform them. In parentheses, you'll see numerous songs you can reference that contain these chord progressions. Do a little digging, listen to these songs and see if you recognize where those progressions happen. Are there other songs you know that have them too?

1) **IV–iv–I**, Twinge of Sadness Progression
(Bruno Mars "When I Was Your Man," Bob Dylan's "Make You Feel My Love," Sara Bareilles' "Manhattan")

2) ♭**VII–IV–I**, Classic Rock Progression
(Grateful Dead "Scarlet Begonias," Roy Orbison's "You Got It," The Beatles' "With a Little Help From My Friends," Rolling Stone's "Wild Horses")

3) ♭**VI**–♭**VII**–**I**, Heroic Progression
(Whitney Houston's 1991 Super Bowl National Anthem, arr. by John Clayton and Ricky Minor, The Who's "Quadrophenia," John Williams' "Superman Theme")

4) **I**–**v**, Sophisticated Songwriter Progression
(James Taylor's "Fire and Rain," Brandi Carlisle's "The Joke")

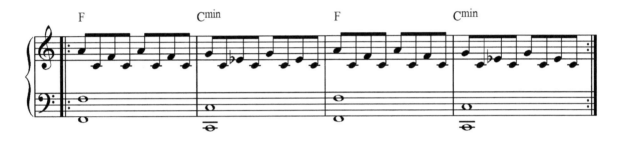

5) **III**–**IV**, Hip Songwriter Chromatic Progression
(David Bowie's "Space Oddity," Otis Redding's "Sittin' on the Dock of the Bay")

6) **I**–♭**II**, Emotional Rock/R&B Progression
(Radiohead's "Everything in its Right Place," India Arie's "This Love")

7) vi–II–IV/V–I, Soulful Cadence Progression
(Chicago's "Saturday in the Park," The Beatles' "Blackbird," Stevie Wonder's "Isn't She Lovely," John Mayer's "Daughters")

Assignment

Perform at least one of the progressions above with a play-along track.

Composition

Compose your own 4-bar chord progressions using non-diatonic chords. Just write in chord symbols above slashes.

1)

2)

LogicPro Application

Now is another good opportunity to create a track with LogicPro. Choose one of your four bar progressions and record it on LogicPro.

To reduce or increase the challenge, add constraints such as composing in specific key(s), using specific techniques, composing more bars (8, 12, 16…) or less bars (2 bars repeating).

Section Review

Skills
Play progressions using modal borrowing.
Play progressions using temporary modulation.
Play progressions using secondary dominants.

Terminology
Non-diatonic
Modal borrowing
Temporary modulation
Secondary dominants

Assignments
Transpose common modal borrowing progressions.
Write out major and minor diatonic chords in F.
Perform a non-diatonic jam with a play-along track.
Compose at least two 4-bar progressions, using non-diatonic chords.
Record your original composition using LogicPro.

6th and 7th chords

6th chords

Major and Minor 6th chords are, for the most part, a dated sound. They were common in jazz and show tunes throughout the first half of the twentieth century. Many of those songs are still classics that we know and love. Minor 6th's still show up once in a while in popular music, but major 6th's are very rare. There is one harmonic context in particular that both major and minor 6th chords are still used in popular music, and that is on the **IV** (or **iv**) chord.

6th chords can be voiced by simply adding the 6th (a whole step above the natural 5th) to a triad. Also, the 6th can be played without the 5th (or instead of the 5th). And in any voicing that works for a 7th chord, the 7th can be lowered to the 6th.

Lenny Kravitz's 1991 hit, "It Ain't Over 'til It's Over," is a good example of a cliché chord progression that contains both the major **IV**⁶ and minor **iv**⁶ (the "twinge of sadness" chord!).

1) 6th Chord Jam in C major

2) 6th Chord Jam in C minor

Assignment

Perform at least one of the above piano parts with a play-along track.

7th chords

So now, let's take a look at 7th chords on paper. If your knowledge of chords is well established, you can probably take this in visually and intellectually, but regardless of your prior knowledge, I can't stress enough how important it is that you go through this stuff on the keyboard.

7th chords, like 6th chords, have been used in popular music for over a century. However, 7th chords continue to be used commonly in many styles, including jazz, R&B, funk, pop, songs for film and theatre, etc. 7th chords are everywhere–sometimes obvious, sometimes as a result of combining chords and bass notes, or sometimes just as a passing tension.

To start playing 7th chords on the piano, follow these steps:
1) Play a major triad in root position with your RH and the root with the LH.
2) In your mind, number the notes of the chord: 1-3-5. Play the 1 with your thumb. For example, play a D♭ major triad: D♭ - F - A♭

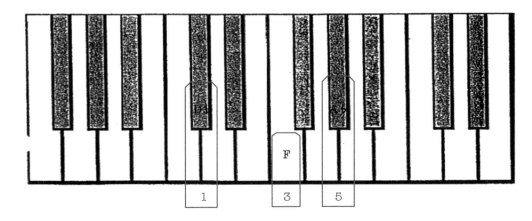

NOTE: If you need to be in a simpler key at this point, that's fine...use C major if you need to. Ideally, though, you can play any of the 12 major triads now without hesitation.

3) Whatever chord you're playing, think of the major scale that correlates: 1-2-3-4-5-6-7
4) Understand that the major 7 is one half step below the 1.
Identify the note name. For example, "The 7 of D♭ is C."

5) Then, drop your RH thumb (the 1) down a half step to the 7. Keep the root in the LH.
6) Play this chord solidly with both hands.

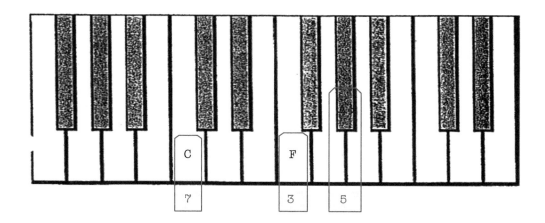

7) In your mind, number the notes of the chord: 7-3-5. (And 1 in the LH.)
8) Understand that you are now playing a major 7th chord.
9) Write the chord symbol. For example, D♭ maj7.
10) Speak the chord symbol. For example, "D flat major seven."

Take your hands off the keyboard and try it again, with only these steps:
1) Decide on a major 7th chord you want to play, and write the chord symbol.
2) Without putting your hands on the piano, visualize the major triad in root position, and then visualize the 7-3-5 voicing.
3) Count off, and play the chord. Hit it and hold it. Make sure it looks, feels, and sounds right.

Do this as many times as you need to until you feel some sense of mastery—the ability to accurately anticipate and flawlessly execute your goal.

Practice: Transpose
Call keys randomly and play a major 7th chord with the RH on the 7-3-5 voicing and LH on the root.

7th Chord Jams

1) maj 7 chords a whole step apart

2) maj 7 chords a fourth apart

3) ♭IIImaj7 ♭IImaj7 Imaj7

Assignment

Perform at least one of the above piano parts with a play-along track.

Pro Tips from Dr. Peter

Chord Voicings: Resonance and Geography

As you learned in Workbook I, the term chord "voicing" refers to the physical order of the notes of a chord. Triads, for instance, can be voiced in root position (1-3-5), or first inversion (3-5-1), or second inversion (5-1-3). Or they can be spread out further, such as 1-5-3. I'll address spread voicings in a more advanced workbook...

What's important for you to retain at this point is the concept of chord voicings being vehicles that exist in different places, and each place has its own particular resonance—literally, it's own "vibe." So, when you play a 7th chord in root position, the resonance of 1-3-5-7 gives a specific impression based on the vibration between those notes that are each a third apart from the next. When you play a 7-3-5 voicing, you get a bit more open resonance—the 7 to the 3 is a fourth, and the root now has to be played a octave lower, which opens up even more resonant space between notes.

Just for fun, I like to think of voicings as "area codes." The 7-3-5 area code has a particularly professional and classy vibe. Think about if you were going to a classy club or restaurant in a nice area of a city—you would probably want to dress up a little, and plan a nice night on the town.

Creating or performing chord progressions is similar—if you want to sound pedestrian and casual, root position chords work great. If you want to sound a little more sophisticated, start using inversions and voicings such as 7-3-5. You will immediately elevate your sound to a more professional level.

Which voicings you choose may vary from song to song, or even section to section. Just be cognizant of what choice you're making, and the impression that creates. You know, some nights you want to wear ripped jeans and go to the taco truck, and others you want to take a date to a fancy restaurant. It's up to you!

Memorize 7th Chord Formulas and Transpose

We need to unpack the 7th chord voicings a little more for you to be able to apply them universally. You have to know what kind of 7 you're looking for, and that depends on the chord type. Memorize these formulas, ASAP:

- Major 7 (e.g., C^{maj7}) = major 3 and major 7

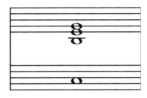

- Dominant 7 (e.g., C^7) = major 3 and flat 7 (aka minor 7)

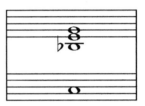

- Minor 7 (e.g., C^{min7}) = flat 3 (aka minor 3) and flat 7 (aka minor 7)

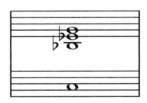

NOTE: It is important to remember that a "flat 3" means that the major third is being lowered by a half step, and a "flat 7" means that the major seventh is being lowered by a half step.

In the key of D major, for instance, the major seventh is C♯. Therefore, the minor seventh, or flat 7, is C natural. *In the analysis of chord tones, the term "flat" really refers to the action of lowering a note.*

Assignment

Play a major 7, dominant 7, and minor 7 chord in the 7-3-5 area code in all 12 keys.

7th Chord Shapes & Sounds

7th chords add layers of complexity that can make music richer, but at the same time make execution more difficult. Certainly, the theory of 7th chords is a deep study that could fill a book by itself. My objectives for you in these sections on 7th chords are to learn:

- fundamental, professional-quality voicings
- effective ways to navigate typical chord progressions
- typical 7th chords in major and minor keys
- typical variations of 7th chords
- contextual examples you can jam on

This section will open a Pandora's box of complexity and possibilities. You need to practice these shapes and progressions in order to gain some control over them. But even more importantly, *you need to have meaningful contexts in which to apply your knowledge and skills.* The real purpose of learning all this stuff is not to master 7th chords completely, but rather to be able to understand, to play, and even to write songs that have 7th chords in them, without being overwhelmed or lost. And the point is also to appreciate 7th chords—the depth and interest they bring to harmony—and to become familiar with their sounds and shapes so they become less like some foreign food you've never wanted to try, and more like great recipes that you can execute to perfection and spices that you can use your imagination with to create new flavor combinations.

Voicings

You have now learned the 7-3-5 voicing (or "area code," as I like to call it). You need to experience constructing those different types of 7th chords in different shape groups. And you need to be very familiar with the difference between major 7th, minor 7th, dominant 7th, diminished 7th chords. Often, the difference is just one note being a half step down or up—all of a sudden it's a very different chord. There's no room for guessing—if you play a major 7 instead of a dominant 7, it will sound horrible. So—deep breath—get ready to do some shedding.

With every 7th chord you learn, it can be valuable to play a root position: 1-3-5-7. But root position 7th chords sound clunky and trite, so I'm not even going to spend time on them here. I want you to learn to play every 7th chord in a 7-3-5 voicing as your default, and expand from there. Pros play 7-3-5, not root position. Once in a while there's a good example of a root position 7th chord in a song, but the instances are few and far between.

7th Chords in the 7-3-5 Area Code
Major, Dominant, Minor, Diminished

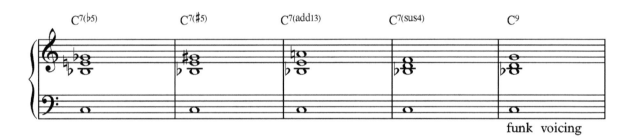

Common Minor Variations

Common Dominant Variations

funk voicing

Common Major Variations

pop voicing

Assignment

Choose at least one voicing variation and transpose to 12 keys.

Assignment

Play through each of the above voicings with the RH, and with the LH playing the roots.

Diatonic 7ᵗʰ Chords

Let's take a different approach now and look at 7ᵗʰ chords in the scale correlating to the key—just as we did with diatonic triads. Start in the key of C major.

    1) Play a C major triad in root position with your RH

    2) Drop the C (the "1") down a half step to B (the "7")

    3) Still play the root of the chord in the LH

    4) Go up through the C major scale with both hands, keeping the 7-3-5 shape

    5) Name the chords consciously as you go, and listen closely to the sounds

Assignment

Write out and play the diatonic 7ᵗʰ chords in all 12 keys, using 7-3-5 voicings.

Use the key of C above as a template. Each key should follow the same pattern: I^{maj7}, ii^{min7}, iii^{min7}, IV^{maj7}, V^7, vi^{min7}, $vii^{min7(b5)}$

Diatonic 7th Chords in the 7-3-5 "Area Code"

Diatonic 7th Chord Progressions

There are a slew of great songs that utilize straightforward diatonic 7th chord progressions. Many, however, have tasteful variations. We will examine typical progressions and variations in the next section. But at this point, just experiment with what you have.

Composition

Choose a key, play through the diatonic 7th chords in the 7-3-5 "area code," and then put together a chord progression that you like. The chords might go up the scale or down the scale; they might jump up or jump down; they might start on the **I**, or start on any other chord in the scale. Experiment, and let your ear tell you what you like and don't like.

Write one or two chords per bar. Write chord symbols over slashes. Then analyze the chords relative to the key, and write in Roman numerals next to the chord symbols. Write each progression in a different key.

Example Progression in F

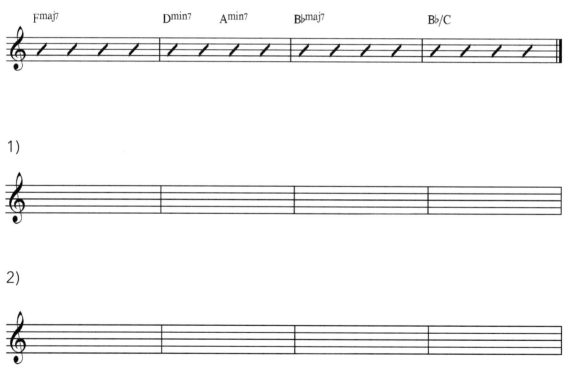

1)

2)

Section Review

Skills

Play progressions using 6th chords.

Play progressions using 7th chords.

Memorize the formulas for major, dominant, and minor 7th chords.

Transpose 7th chords to all 12 keys, playing 7-3-5 voicings in the RH, roots in the LH.

Terminology

6th chords

7th chords

7-3-5 voicing

Major 7th chord

Dominant 7th chord

Minor 7th chord

Assignments

Perform a piano part using 6th chords with a play-along track.

Perform a piano part using 7th chords with a play-along track.

Play a major, dominant, and minor 7th chord in the 7-3-5 voicing in 12 keys.

Transpose a 7th chord variation in the 7-3-5 voicing to all keys.

Play major 7th chords in 7-3-5 voicings in all keys, organized by shape group.

Write out diatonic 7th chords in 7-3-5 voicings in all keys.

Compose at least two 4-bar progressions, using diatonic 7th chords.

The ii – V

You really can't study 7th chords without discussing **ii** - **V** progressions. In the key of C major, a **ii** - **V** progression is…?

Think it through, if you don't already know it. C is the **I**, D is the **ii** , etc. So a **ii** - **V** is: D^{min7} G^7

NOTE: The dash in the **ii** - **V** is just to show movement from one chord to the next. It is not an important part of analysis.

Remember how the **V** chord leads back to the **I**? Well, the **ii** leads to the **V**. So, a **ii** - **V** progression gives you a double layer of tension and resolution–the ii has tension that resolves to the **V**, which has its own tension that wants to resolve to the **I** (primarily). All this tension and resolution is what helps make music flavorful.

The Secret Formula

Now, you can play a D^{min7} and G^7 in the 7-3-5 "area code," but that requires jumping the chord a fourth up or fifth down from D to G, and it will get harder once you move to other keys with black notes. I'm going to give you the secret formula for playing **ii** - **V** progressions–this is how you avoid jumping around, and sound like a pro moving from the **ii** to the **V**.

The secret formula is…

Drop the sizzle of the tizzle down a hizzle.

That's right. Say it out loud. Don't be shy. We're allowed a little fun in the midst of all this complicated stuff.

But what does it mean to drop the sizzle of the tizzle down a hizzle?!

Translation: "Drop the seven of the two down a half step." On paper, that should actually be: Drop the 7 of the **ii** down a half step.

NOTE: Remember, in analysis, we're using *Arabic numerals for numbering single notes* in relation to a chord or key, *and Roman numerals for numbering chords* in relation to a key or tonal center.

Play the **ii** – **V** progression in the key of C as written on the following page. Don't forget to move your LH from D to G. And really get a feel for the 7 of the **ii** going down a half step.

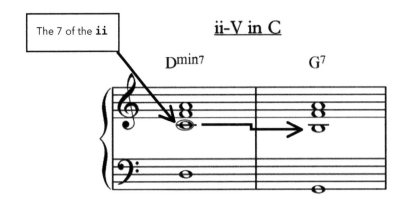

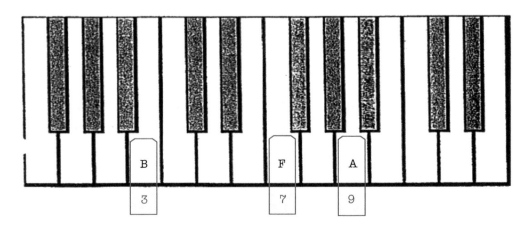

Shortcut the Math

The 7 of D is…?

Instead of counting up from D ("D=1, E=2," etc.), just go to the note below the root. You can always do that to find the 7 of a chord. You really don't have time to sit around counting up to 7, anyway. Just go to the note below the root, and that's the 7. The note below D is C. So, in your **ii – V** progression in the key of C, you start with D^{min7} in the 7-3-5 "area code," and then you drop C down a half step to B, move your LH bass note to G, and voila!—a beautiful G^7.

3-7-9 Voicings

There are many, many ways that you can voice 7th chords. The 7-3-5 voicing (aka "area code") is the easiest to find and sound professional with. But you've got to have some variations in your toolbox. And the **ii – V** progression reveals the first variation for you to learn: 3-7-9.

You might have noticed that when you use the secret formula to move from the D^{min7} (RH in the 7-3-5) area code to a G^7, that G^7 is no longer in the 7-3-5.

Take a look at it—it's in the 3-7-9 "area code." (Make sure your LH is playing the root—G.)

Now, if you want to be extremely thorough, you will practice every 7th chord you've played in the 7-3-5 "area code" in a 3-7-9 "area code." I know you might run into trouble with that, though. Finding the 9 can be tricky until you get used to it (it's a whole step above the 1), and seeing the 3-7-9 voicing is more difficult visually because it bears little resemblance to a related triad. And unless you really are ambitious to master this stuff, it's not going to be effective for you to do all the transpositions at this point—that will likely overwhelm your brain.

So what we really need to do is apply some of these new voicings in the contexts of progressions, techniques, and songs.

The ii – V – I

You've played **V** – **I** progressions, and you've played **ii** – **V** progressions. So now we'll play **ii** – **V** – **I**'s.

Just to double check, that is spoken: "Two five one's."

Here is your **ii** – **V** – **I** in the key of C major.

Play it now, and listen to it as you play. It sounds very consonant to resolve to the **I** chord; yet the major 7 gives it a twinge of tension, for sure. If you want a less jazzy, less tense sound, resolve to a C major triad.

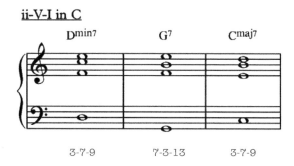

The above **ii** – **V** – **I** starts in a 7-3-5 voicing, but you can also start in a 3-7-9 voicing (or any voicing, for that matter). Check it out:

If this is your first time through this section, this second set of voicings may be a little mystifying. 7-3-13?? Don't worry…it's just one of many variations that you're about to explore. At this point, unless you're particularly motivated to absorb the theory, just don't even think about the "13." All you need to know is the 7-3-5 and the 3-7-9, and how to apply the secret formula for **ii – V** progressions.

PRO TIPS FROM DR. PETER

Just Do It

Your understanding will get deeper and more thorough naturally with repetition. What you really need to focus on going forward is practicing. Take your time to get your fingers on the right notes. Then repeat the physical motions until they are automatic. Make It Easy. The more keys you practice in to the point of automaticity, the more the shapes will become familiar. Once you establish familiarity with the shapes and progressions, then the theoretical understanding has roots to ground into. Listen to Nike: Just Do It. Correctly. Again and again and again…

Practice

Play a **ii – V** progression using the secret formula in all 12 keys. Follow these steps: 1) choose a key, 2) go up a whole step from the tonic to find the root of the **ii** chord, 3) play the root of the **ii** chord with your LH, and a 7-3-5 voicing of the **ii** minor 7, 4) move your LH to the root of the **V**, and drop the sizzle (i.e., drop the seven of the ii down a half-step) in your RH. Repeat this process in a steady tempo, and experiment with what kind of groove you can play the **ii – V** in.

Check off the box next to the key, and try to get all 12!

□ A	□ G
□ B	□ D♭/C♯
□ C	□ E♭/D♯
□ D	□ G♭/F♯
□ E	□ A♭/G♯
□ F	□ B♭/A♯

Assignment

Complete the Major **ii – V – I** worksheet on the following page. Write in the missing notes, and play the progressions using the LH bass line of your choice. Perform and/or record with the **ii – V – I** play-along track.

Major ii-V-I progressions
starting in the 7-3-5 area code

in C:

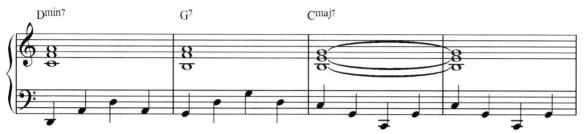

in Db:

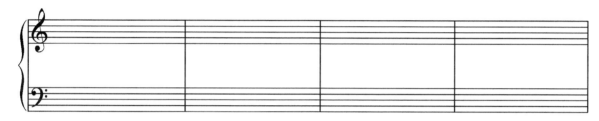

in D:

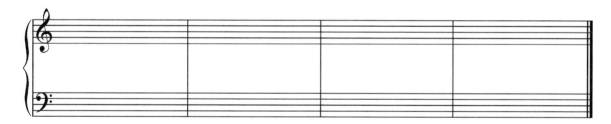

If you want to sound more jazzy, try these walking bass line variations:

Diatonic Walking Bass Line

Chromatic Walking Bass Line

Section Review

Skills

Play and transpose **ii** − **V** progressions using the secret formula.
Perform **ii** − **V** − **I** progressions in various keys with LH bass walking bass lines.

Terminology

ii − **V** progressions
The secret formula for **ii** − **V**'s: "Drop the seven of the two down a half step"
3-7-9 voicings

Assignments

Play **ii** − **V** progressions using the secret formula, and transpose to multiple keys.
Write **ii** − **V** − **I** progressions in various keys.

Advanced Applications of 7th Chords

This section will mirror the work you did with non-diatonic triads and voicing the melody with triads, culminating in a handful of piano parts for you to play, and a chance for you to compose something.

Non-Diatonic 7th Chords

Now that you've entered the world of 7th chords on the piano, you should expand past diatonic harmony. You can apply the same strategies with 7th chords as you did with triads–modal borrowing, temporary modulation, and secondary dominants.

Modal Borrowing

Since C major and C minor are really the easiest keys to visually and physically feel the difference between major and minor, we will work there initially again. But remember, transposing to other keys is crucial if you want to gain some mastery over this stuff. The primary challenge, once you understand the theory here, is to get physically familiar with the shapes of these chords in different keys on the instrument. Does that sound familiar? It should.

NOTE: As you play through these chords, make sure you play the root in your LH. For instance, for Cmaj7, you will play C in your LH and B-E-G in your RH.

Diatonic 7th chords in C major

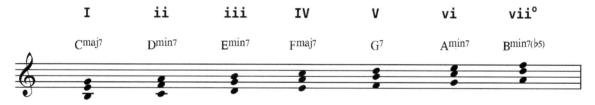

Diatonic 7th chords in C minor

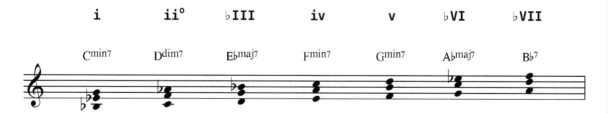

Practice: Major key, borrowing from Minor key

1) **I** - **vi** versus **I** - ♭**VI**

Play a Cmaj7, then an Amin7. Play Cmaj7, then A♭maj7.

2) **I** - **iv** versus **I** - **iv**

Play Cmaj7, then Fmaj7. Play Cmaj7, then Fmin7.

3) **I** - **iii** versus **I** - ♭**III**

Play Cmaj7, then Emin7. Play Cmaj7, then E♭maj7.

Practice: Minor key, borrowing from Major key

1) **i** - **v** versus **i** - **V**

Play a Cmin7, then a Gmin7 triad. Play Cmin7, then G7.

2) **i** - **iv** versus **i** - **IV**

Play Cmin7, then Fmin7. Play Cmin7, then Fmaj7.

3) **i** - ♭**VII** versus **i** - **vii**

Play Cmin7, then B♭maj7. Play Cmin7, then Bmin7(♭5).

Practice: Transpose

Transpose the above practice examples, and play them on cue.

Assignment

Write out the major and minor key diatonic 7th chords in F—note names and chord symbols. Write in the key signature, or write in each accidental as they appear in the chords.

| I | ii | iii | IV | V | vi | vii° |

| i | ii° | ♭III | iv | v | ♭VI | ♭VII |

Temporary Modulation

The leading tone slash chord is probably my favorite vehicle for changing keys. However, 7th chords can be very effective as well. You can easily create a pleasing cadence to a new key by inserting a **V - I** progression or a **ii - V - I**. Play through the examples below to get a taste of 7th chords creating temporary modulations.

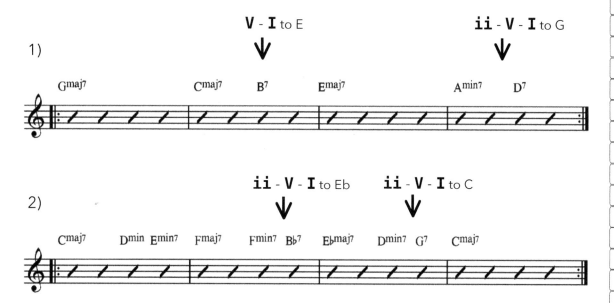

Assignment

Perform and/or record at least one of the above progressions live with a play-along track.

Secondary Dominants

You may be wondering, "what is the difference between using a **V - I** progression to create a temporary modulation versus secondary dominants?" The way I think of it is this: temporary modulation is created by a cadence to a tonic *outside of the key*. Secondary dominants, on the other hand, are related to diatonic chords–e.g., the **V**7 of the **ii**–and therefore resolve back into the original key.

1) **III** to the **vi** Jam in D

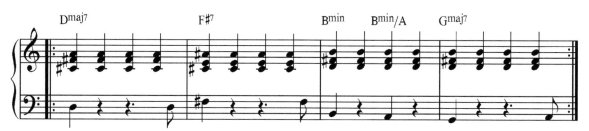

2) **I** to the **IV** Jam in D ♭

3) **VI** to the **ii** Jam in F

Assignment

Perform and/or record at least one of the above jams live with a play-along track.

Voicing the Melody with 7th Chords

You may have noticed in some of these examples, I have used not only 7-3-5 voicings–sometimes it works well to have inversions of those voicings, in order to have smoother voice leading, or to use a 3-7-9 voicing. There is nothing wrong with playing a 7th chord in a 3-5-7 voicing or 5-7-3. The only reason we aren't spending more time practicing those inversions is because I don't want to overwhelm your brain. The 7-3-5 is the easiest voicing to locate, because it is so close to a 1-3-5 (root position) triad, and the 7-3-5 sounds *professional*, so it should become your default.

That said, you can use inversions of 7th chords in the same way you use them for triads: 1) to create smooth voice leading, and 2) to voice the melody. Do you remember what "voicing the melody" means? It means to use the top note of your chord voicing(s) to match or create a melody. Contemporary pianists such as Alicia Keys and Regina Spektor do a particularly nice job of creating piano parts in this way. I recommend you check out their music, along with classic rockers like Elton John, and Michael McDonald (the Doobie Brothers), and contemporary R&B star Brian McKnight.

Play through the examples below to get a taste of the sophistication that using 7th chords to voice a melody can bring to a piano part.

1) Gospel Jam

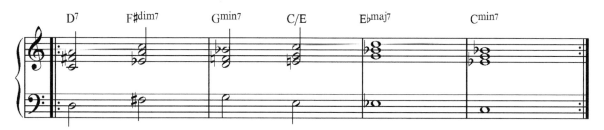

2) R&B/Pop Songwriter Jam

3) Contemporary R&B Jam

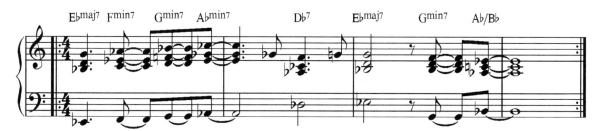

4) Jazzy Songwriter Jam

Assignment

    Perform and/or record at least one of the above jams live with a play-along track.

Composition

Choose a key, and consciously experiment with diatonic and non-diatonic 7th chords. Write out both hands (the grand staff) for a piano part. Use at least one non-diatonic 7th chord in each progression. Try to create a melodic top line, and voice the melody with your chords. Write chord symbols over the staff.

1)

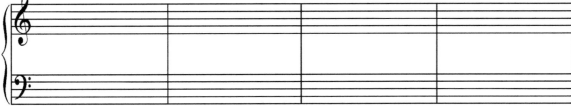

2)

PRO TIPS FROM DR. PETER

7th Chords = Jazziness

Entering the world of 7th chords basically equates to entering the world of jazz. Certainly, using one 7th chord doesn't mean that a song is now a jazz song. You wouldn't call Elton John or John Legend songs jazz. You wouldn't even call Stevie Wonder's music jazz. However, in their songs that have 7th chords, you can distinctly hear some bit of "jazziness."

Think of jazziness as a spectrum. On one side of the spectrum is no jazziness, and on the other side is total jazziness. You can map a relatively direct correlation between the number of 7th chords and the amount of jazziness–the more 7th chords, the more jazziness. Think about that when you listen to music. Which songs, which artists, which genres, incorporate the most jazziness?

Section Review

Skills
Apply non-diatonic strategies with 7th chord progressions.
Play grand staff piano parts using non-diatonic 7th chords.
Play grand staff piano parts using 7th chords to voice the melody.

Terminology
Non-diatonic
Modal borrowing
Temporary modulation
Secondary dominants
Voicing the melody

Assignments
Transpose modal borrowing progressions.
Write out diatonic 7th chords in F major and F minor.
Perform and/or record piano parts using secondary dominants.
Perform and/or record piano parts voicing the melody with 7th chords.
Compose at least two 4-bar progressions, using non-diatonic 7th chord.

The Blues with 7th Chords

In section 10 of Workbook I, you were introduced to the 12-bar blues. Now, it's time to apply 7th chords to the blues, and play on the jazzier side of the spectrum. In Workbook III, you will have the opportunity to expand on this harmonic template, by adding altered dominant chords and extended **ii - V** progressions.

Below, you'll see a blues progression with a LH walking bass line and RH 7th chords using 7-3-5 voicings. In the last bar, there is a **ii - V** that will take you back to the top of the form to repeat. That **ii - V** does *not* work well as an ending, though. If you need to keep it simple at the end, just play C7 and hold it in the last bar. However, if you want to get more sophisticated, use the ending I've written out for you below—just insert those two bars into the last two bars of the form. It'll take a little practicing, but it's worth it if you can get it!

Sophisticated Blues Ending

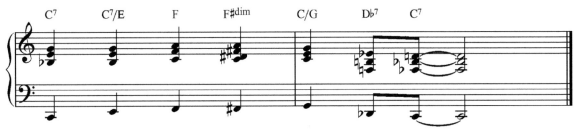

69

Blues Play-Along

Choose your blues play-along mp3, insert it into LogicPro, and play along with an acoustic piano sound. Get as close as you can to executing the progression and techniques written on the previous page. Bounce an mp3 of the full track.

Practice: Transpose

Play a 12-bar blues, like the one above, in the key of F. Write in the chord symbols (above the bars with slashes in them) for a 12-bar blues in the key of F, and play the same 7-3-5 voicings as you did in the key of C.

1) Key of F

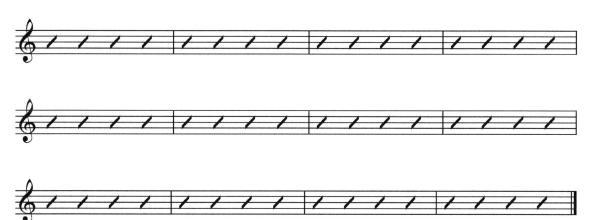

Blues Scale Improvisation

In Workbook I, you worked on bluesy improvisation. You can use all of that knowledge and skill again any time you improvise over a blues! I'm not going to rehash it all here. Instead, I'm going to give you some new vocabulary using the "blues scale." When you play a blues in the key of C, you can use the C blues scale over the entire form of the song, even when the chord is F7, or G7. Just remember, if you play a blues in the key of F, you need to use the F blues scale.

Try playing these short lines below, and then try making up your own short lines. Then open your LogicPro Blues Play-Along project, and record yourself improvising over that. Have fun!

C Blues Scale:

Assignment

Write your own blues lines

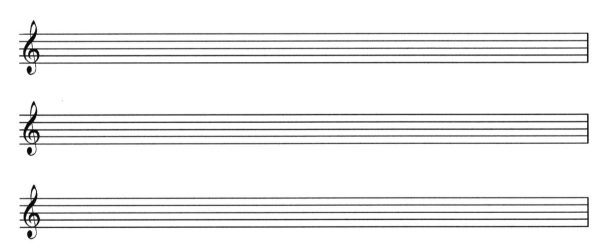

Assignment: Complete your Blues Play-Along

Open your Blues Play-Along LogicPro project, and create a new track that will be your improvisation track. Assign a sound—piano, electric piano, or organ will work. Improvise along with your recording using the blues scale for a while. When you feel ready, record!

1) Bounce an mp3 file of your project.

2) Sit back and listen and enjoy!

Pro Tips from Dr. Peter

Improvisation is Story-telling

When you improvise, you are essentially having a spontaneous conversation, using the language of music, in the dialect (or musical style) of the song. Think, for a moment, about what makes a good conversation—when are you compelled to listen to what someone is saying? There is nothing more attention-grabbing than a good story, whether it is non-fiction or fiction. A story needs a character that you can get invested in. Each idea you play is like a new character. And a good story doesn't just have an endless line of characters. You have to get to know characters, and how they interact with each other. You do this in improvisation through repetition and variation of ideas. This is called "motivic development." Before you introduce a new idea, try repeating your first idea. Try extending it or contracting it, or changing the rhythm. Move it up an octave or down an octave. Repetition and variation then become like a character's back-story, or their plot lines. Once that is established, you can bring in a new character, or musical motif, and have it interact with the original idea.

In this way, you both create a more compelling improvisation to hear, and you take the pressure off of yourself to constantly think of something new to play. In fact, many great improvisations use a simple idea, repeating and varying it for extended periods of time. Try it! Think of each idea as a character in your story. Be stingy with creating brand new characters. Give each character life with repetition, and depth with variation.

Section Review

Skills

Play a 12-bar blues with 7th chords in 7-3-5 voicings.
Play RH blues scale phrases.
Compose and improvise RH lines using the C blues scale.
Transpose the blues chord progression.

Terminology

Blues scale
Motivic development

Assignments

Record a 12-bar blues in LogicPro with a play-along track.
Transpose a 12-bar blues progression to the key of F.
Compose your own blues scale phrases.

Closing Words

Independent Learning

The end goal here is that you are able and inspired to seek out music that you want to learn, and successfully tackle it. That begins with listening. Perhaps you spend time just imitating a recording, trying to learn by ear. Perhaps you find sheet music or a chord chart. Perhaps you combine the use of notation and your ear. When I learn songs, it's almost always some combination of the two.

Then, you just need to:
1) Make time to practice.
2) Work out the techniques and challenges.
3) Make it easy, by practicing with robotic repetition and precision.
4) And then play for someone—a friend, a family member, a classmate.

There are many pertinent questions, and you can expect to have to ask more than one of them—from "Where do I find chord charts?" to "How do I fit my fingers on this chord?"

Part of independent learning is seeking information when problems arise—your teacher, your peers, and oftentimes a friend named Google, have the answers. If you have an unanswered question, or if you're stuck on a challenge, ask for help.

Each one of the four steps listed above can be frustrating, difficult, or even scary. Sometimes getting help is the only way through. You can do it! There is no doubt.

After my sophomore year of high school, I was 16 years old, and for the first time in 5 years I decided not to go baseball camp in the summer. Instead, I took a leap and spent eight weeks at Interlochen Arts Camp. It was there that I realized that being a musician was the path I wanted. My peers were incredible musicians—far more advanced than I was in many respects. I was humbled. But my peers were also incredible people. The two jazz pianists ahead of me took me under their wing in different ways—teaching me how to practice, how to voice chords, how to be a stronger improviser. The great jazz pianist, Donald Vega, was 18 at the time, and the top pianist in the camp. I'll never forget one day when I walked by the practice sheds and stopped to listen to him. He looked up and saw me and invited me in. Donald is a generous and very kind man, as anyone who knows him will attest—but he was 18, and I was "competition." Instead of "vibing" me, Donald showed me what he was practicing—we played for each other, and he gave me advice on what to work on. His actions that day taught me how great being in a community of musicians can be. Sometimes you know what your questions are and sometimes you don't, but if you seek out the people who are at the next level, you are likely to find someone willing to devote their time and energy to helping you progress.

Someday, you could be that someone, helping others.

Addendum 1: Scales

Learning To Play Scales

To begin learning scales, learn one major scale from each shape group–
B, C, D♭, and D.

B major scale – RH two octaves up and down, LH hit and hold the tonic

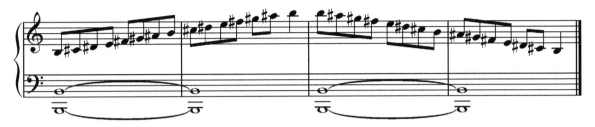

Shapes in a Scale

Let's take a visual and physical approach to the scale now.

There are always two finger patterns in a major scale–a <u>1-2-3</u> and a <u>1-2-3-4</u>. That's <u>thumb-index-middle</u>, <u>thumb-index-middle-ring</u>. I repeat, there are always those two finger patterns in a major scale. Once you find them, and practice them systematically, scales in every key become manageable. Take a look at the visual below:

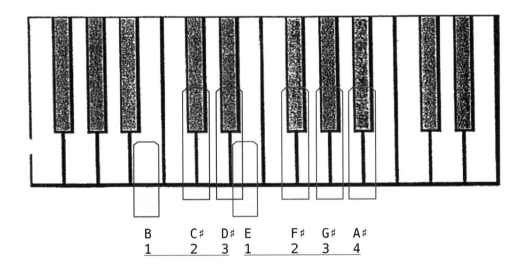

B	C♯	D♯	E	F♯	G♯	A♯
1	2	3	1	2	3	4

Four Step Process
Step 1 - Clusters

In this case, I think it actually helps to have the black notes in the scale. Look at how nicely that all falls under the fingers, with the thumb on B, and then on E again. Take your <u>1-2-3</u> fingers and hold them in front of you. Now play <u>B-C♯-D♯</u> simultaneously as a three-note cluster. Then add the ring finger so you have your <u>1-2-3-4</u> fingers and hold those in front of you. Now play <u>E-F♯-G♯-A♯</u> simultaneously as a four-note cluster. Program the two shapes into your fingers.

Play them up and down the piano. Recognize that these are the notes in the key of B major.

When you shift up and down the keyboard, your hand should be like a typewriter–moving horizontally. Don't lift your hand way up in the air. Don't wiggle your fingers around searching for notes. Just hold your cluster shape(s) and move left or right.

Can you take your hand off the keyboard, turn away, clear your mind, and then turn back to the keyboard with the intention of playing the notes in the key of B and play those two cluster shapes right away? Once you can do that, move on to Step 2.

Step 2 – Scale Clusters

Now play the three-note group one note at a time. You can conceive of the notes as:

- 1-2-3
- Do-Re-Mi
- B-C♯-D♯
- Thumb-Index-Middle

Ideally, you can mentally toggle between these ways of conceiving the notes. But ultimately, all that really matters is what you do. Are your fingers playing the right notes? Can you replicate it on demand? Once the answer is yes, you are ready for Step 3.

But first, play the 1-2-3-4 group one note at a time as well.

After you have played each group alone a few times, play 1-2-3, pause, and 1-2-3-4, pause, 1-2-3, pause, 1-2-3-4. Up two octaves and finish with your RH pinky on B.

Then you have to practice going down: 4-3-2-1, 3-2-1, 4-3-2-1, 3-2-1. Don't skip this step. Going down feels different than up the scale, and those shapes need to be in your fingers (and in your ears).

Step 3 – Bridging the Gaps

Everyone wants to skip Step 3. Don't do it. I promise you, if you follow the steps in order, the scales will become easy for you with consistent practice, and you won't have to think through every note. You will have the shapes in the scales programmed for automaticity. And then you can just enjoy playing.

Step 3 is just adding one note to each cluster, in order to conquer the challenge of crossing fingers over and under. This is where the typewriter thing really comes into play. The ideal crossover does not stretch or contort the fingers or wrist. Your whole hand just slides horizontally. The crossover happens, but the other fingers just whip right into place, and your wrist rotates minimally compared to what you might do otherwise. This is one of those things that really needs a demonstration. Watch the video of me walking you through the four steps of learning scales.

Step 4 – Playing through it

At this point, you should be ready to play the whole scale. Everyone wants to start at this step. But I'm telling you, if you discipline your practice to go step by step, every scale will become relatively easy.

Step 4 is just playing the scale from the bottom to the top and back down again, smoothly and with good hand position. Make the notes as even as you can. I recommend practicing these scales with a metronome, beginning with a tempo goal of: quarter note = 72.

Fulcrums

While we're on the topic of mechanics, we need to cover fulcrums. Fulcrums are what give you power on the instrument. Power without strain. I wish someone had showed me this before I blew out my chops and got tendonitis when I was 20 years old. But that experience certainly provided me with the motivation to change, and to seek wise counsel.

The fulcrum concept comes from the legendary piano pedagogue, Abby Whiteside, and her tome, *The Indispensables of Piano Playing*. The 1-2-3, 1-2-3-4 application of it comes from the late great Charlie Banacos, Boston's jazz guru for three decades. Charlie completely transformed my relationship to the instrument with this practice.

Don't take it lightly. This is piano Jedi stuff. It will take consistent repetition over time to master. We're going to do this practice using the C major scale. Just like you did in the key of B, find your 1-2-3 and 1-2-3-4 clusters. Remember, 1-2-3 means thumb-index-middle finger, and so on.

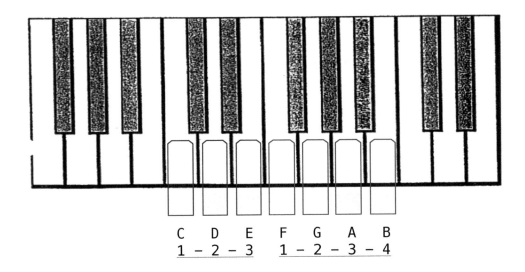

Now, hold out your 1-2-3 finger group in front of you. Starting with your RH thumb on middle C, play the three notes consecutively on the piano in one quick motion. Do the same thing with the 1-2-3-4 group. This exercise is just to be played in one octave at first, but you can expand it to two or three once you get the hang of it. It shouldn't sound like a scale. It's more like two short runs, with a breath in between.

The most important aspect of this exercise is actually not the notes or the fingering, per se. *The most important thing is the motion of your arm,* from your shoulder all the way to your fingers.

1) The driving force should be coming from the rotation of your shoulder
2) The rotation of your shoulder pushes your arm forward
3) The forward motion of your arm makes your wrist bend slightly upward
4) Maintain a relaxed wrist and good hand position, while letting the power transfer all the way from the shoulder through the arm to the fingers

The larger the fulcrum, the greater the power. Look at your finger fulcrums (aka knuckles). They're so much smaller than the wrist, which is smaller than the elbow, which is smaller than the shoulder. *The larger the fulcrum, the greater the power.* In fact, the largest fulcrum is the waist. Consciously or not, many great pianists sway at the waist while playing. Done correctly, this can access even greater power–the entire torso propels energy into the fingers!

For now, though, just focus on getting the arm to push forward as the shoulder rotates, and channel that force into your fingers. Done correctly, this will take most of the strain off of your fingers, and open up your body's ability to play with power, precision, and ease.

In addition to the practice above, you can approach the C major scale in the same manner as B major.
Step 1 – clusters
Step 2 – scale clusters
Step 3 – bridging the gaps
Step 4 – the whole thing

Fingerings

Take a look at the Db major scale now. The most significant difference between it and the B, C, and D, is that it starts on a black note. And RH thumbs don't take kindly to black notes. In fact, when playing scales, you want to pretty much avoid thumbs on black notes altogether. No thumbs on black notes. NOTE: there are plenty of instances when you will play black notes with your thumb, just not in scales. At some point, if you're studying to become a virtuoso pianist, you may want to play all 12 scales with the same fingering. But that's a long way from here. So...*no thumbs on black notes.*

This means that a D♭ major scale doesn't start with the thumb! Uh-oh. But D♭ still has a 1-2-3 and 1-2-3-4. Can you find them? Remember, thumb goes on white notes.

Ok, so the 1-2-3 is actually C-D♭-E♭. And the 1-2-3-4 is F-G♭-A♭-B♭. So the scale starts with 2—your index finger. Still, you should practice your D♭ major scale in the same way as B and C.

Step 1 - clusters

Step 2 - scale clusters

Step 3 - bridging the gaps

Step 4 - the whole thing

When you get to Step 4, just don't play the C with your thumb—start the scale on D♭ with your index finger, and you're off and running.

The D major scale is back in the familiar 1-2-3, 1-2-3-4 group where the thumb actually begins the scale. Don't forget to practice Step 3 with care on the way down the scales as well. The 4-3-2-1 crossover trips a lot of people up. I've seen many a fingering fall apart on the way down a scale.

81

Major Scales

Assignment

Find the 1-2-3 and 1-2-3-4 groups, and practice each scale in the manner outlined in the previous section.

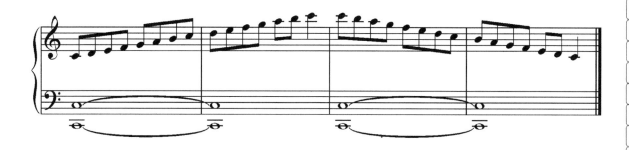

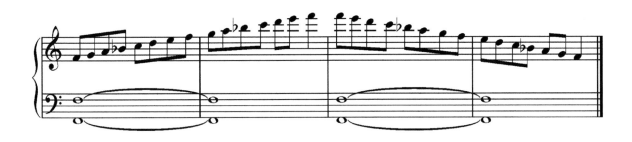

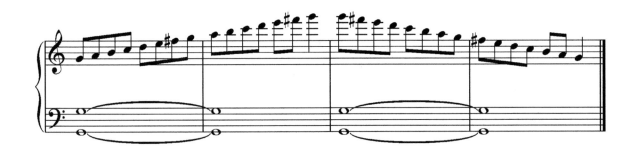

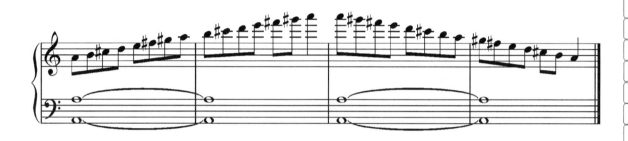

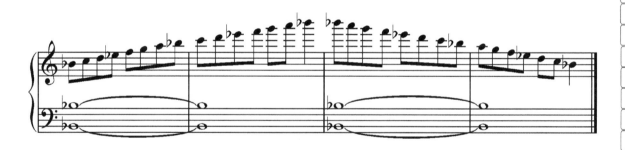

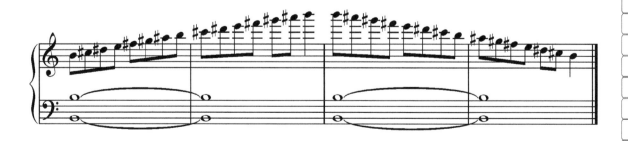

Natural Minor Scales

Assignment

Find the 1-2-3 and 1-2-3-4 groups, and practice each scale in the manner outlined previously.

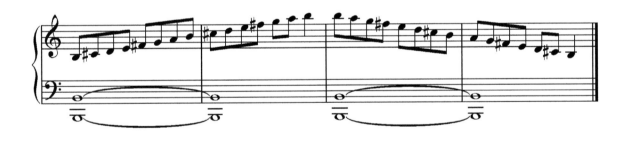

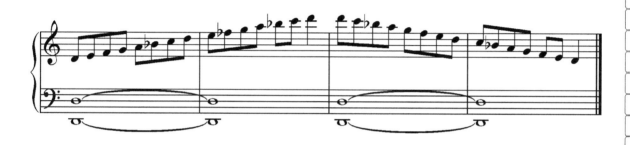

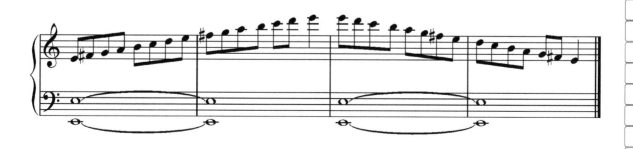

Two Hand Scales

Adding your LH makes scales 100% more difficult. But understanding the scale learning method, and knowing the notes of scales in all keys mitigates the difficulty to some extent.

The LH can learn scales with exactly the same four step process as the RH. However, the LH is looking for <u>3-2-1</u> and <u>4-3-2-1</u> clusters on the way up the scale. And they do not correlate with the RH clusters in any easy-to-remember way. Below, I have labeled the clusters in the RH and LH.

NOTE: Many LH scales start on the 4 (ring finger) or 5 (pinky) by necessity. But in the second and third octave, that becomes the 1 (thumb). Also remember, on all of the black note scales the RH always has a thumb on C and F (or C♭ in the key of G♭).

I recommend that you note the clusters on the page as you learn your scales. Happy practicing!

Addendum 2: Sight-Reading

Sight-Reading Method

One of the most common disparities between students' abilities in piano study is in the area of sight-reading. You might be used to learning everything by ear, or you might have studied classical piano for years and be able to read Mozart sonatas. Maybe you never touched a piano before you started this workbook, or maybe you're a great sight-reader on the trumpet, but you've never even looked at bass clef, let alone tried to read treble and bass clef together.

Now, depending on your teacher and your interest, you may learn a lot of music via sheet music, or by chord charts, or you may learn mostly by rote (i.e., just by doing it again and again until you've got it down).

Your primary goal is to execute the music on the piano. If you can sight-read, then you know what it feels like to look at notes on a staff and then put your fingers on the piano and have music come out. It's a very cool experience. Good sight-readers look at the sheet music and play without even looking at the piano.

If sight-reading is a challenge, though, here's what I want you to do:
1) Learn to execute the music however you learn best.
2) Once you are putting your fingers in the right place at the right time, look at the sheet music, and correlate what you're playing to the visual representation of the notes.
3) Do the same thing with chord symbols. Begin with execution, and then stop looking at the keyboard and start looking at the symbols on the page.

During my doctoral studies, a colleague completed a literature review on research into the effectiveness of various sight-reading methods. I'll never forget her presentation, because it surprised me so much. If you're trying to improve sight-reading, the method doesn't matter—the only thing that seems to matter is how much you sight-read. So whatever level you're at, if you just consistently read music the best you can, you'll get better and better at it. That said, learning to sight-read is a cognitive feat that can be approached more strategically than haphazardly.

The following method for learning to sight-read is borrowed directly from my piano guru, Charlie Banacos. When he taught me this method of improving sight-reading, I was already a professional pianist, but I was still a pathetic sight-reader. See, I learned everything by ear and by rote, and eventually by chord charts. I could read single lines in treble clef, because most jazz charts are written that way. But even that was often a struggle. Learning piano music like Bach Inventions or Chopin Etudes was laughably painstaking for me. I did it, piecing things together one little chunk at a time. I still struggle to sight-read grand staff piano music in real time, but the method Charlie gave me revolutionized my relationship to sight-reading, and over time I developed a level of competence that is respectable, at least.

This method does not include standard sight-reading exercises in grand staff. *You should definitely* work on sight-reading piano music in authentic contexts–work from a sight-reading workbook, or just pull up sheet music from various styles. However, this method will help create a cognitive shortcut from your visual perception of the dots on the staves to the motor function of your fingers moving to the correct place on the instrument, which will help your general sight-reading immeasurably.

I can promise you that you will establish a strong foundation for sight-reading on the piano if you follow this method and practice consistently. Combine the practices with actual sight-reading of piano music in tempo. If you want to be thorough, you should combine it with rhythm reading as well (I worked on rhythm flash cards for two years with Charlie Banacos). The rhythm flashcards are included in Commercial Workbook I. If you need a copy of them, however, you can email me and I'll email you a pdf.

Note Reading

Now, on to the Banacos method for note reading…

The awesome thing about this method is that it programs your brain to do precisely what it needs to do in sight-reading, which is to translate the visual stimuli (notes on the staff) into finger motions. Did you get that? When you sight-read, it's about *translating visual into physical*. You don't have to think about what the names of the notes are, what key you're in, or what chord you're playing… You're basically a human "player piano." The motions of your hand correlate directly to the dots on the page. In fact, I want you to not think of the note names when you do this.

Sight-reading is about putting your fingers in the right place–it's geography! Each line and space on the staff represents a note on the piano. Not just a note name, but an actual note–for instance, "middle C" is the first ledger line below the treble clef staff, and the first ledger line above the bass clef staff.

Those aren't just Cs anywhere on the piano, those notes are *middle C.*

Exercise #1

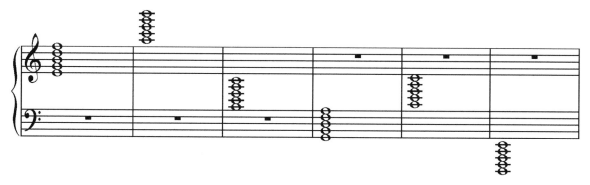

There are three things to play with your RH followed by three with your LH. These are the geographical areas of piano sight-reading—the staff (treble clef and bass clef), and the ledger lines above and below. Play these through in order once or twice every time you sit down at the piano. Every singe time.

This will program your brain to send your hand to that geographical area when it sees notes there. You will be amazed at how much of a difference this makes in sight-reading. Instead of seeing notes and going through a whole thinking process, figuring out the note names and looking for them on the piano—perhaps in the wrong octave—your hand will be moving to the right place automatically.

NOTE: If you can play all five notes—with five fingers—awesome! Most people can't, though. In which case you just need to arpeggiate the "chord" (i.e., play one note at a time). Just do it quickly, so it feels like a group of notes, not one deliberate note at a time. This is not about <u>e</u>very good <u>b</u>oy <u>d</u>oes <u>f</u>ine.

Do this practice religiously. It may take five or even ten minutes the first time. But eventually, you should be able to go through the six "chords" in five to ten seconds. That's your goal. Make it easy.

Random Note Heads Reading Practice

In Workbook II, I am including an expanded section on random note-head sight-reading. I have found that some students are overwhelmed by working with all of the notes in the staff at first, and are aided by honing in on specific groups of notes. The first two pages contain targeted random note-head sight-reading practice, followed by the full staff random note-head reading, and ledger lines above and below the staff.

You can read these notes in tempo or out of tempo. You can read one or two bars, or a whole system. You can read them in treble clef (RH) or bass clef (LH). You can apply a key signature, and read them with one flat, or two sharps, etc. You can even turn the page on its head and read them backwards if they get too familiar.

As much as possible, don't think of the note names! You're programming your brain to translate the visual input into motor actions–visual to physical. Double check your hand to make sure you're in the right octave.

Do this practice religiously also. You may need to start with one bar and then two bars. Your end goal is to play any one of these lines, RH or LH, in less than 30 seconds. Don't spend more than 5 minutes on this practice, but do it every time you sit down at the piano. Every single time.

As you progress through the Banacos method, you can read the worksheet of random note-heads in the ledger lines. After that, you can read the thirds in the staff, and then thirds in ledger lines. You can continue and make your own worksheets of fourths, fifths, sixths, etc.. You can make triad shapes as well. There's no limit to what shapes you use–the point is for your brain to learn to recognize the music and move your fingers to the right place at the right time. Remember that you are programming your eye-brain-finger coordination. Practice regularly, and you will progress.

Assignment

Challenge yourself to practice the reading worksheet every day for four weeks in a row. No more than 5 minutes each time! Set a timer if you're going over.

Wk 1	Wk 2	Wk 3	Wk 4
☐ 1	☐ 1	☐ 1	☐ 1
☐ 2	☐ 2	☐ 2	☐ 2
☐ 3	☐ 3	☐ 3	☐ 3
☐ 4	☐ 4	☐ 4	☐ 4
☐ 5	☐ 5	☐ 5	☐ 5
☐ 6	☐ 6	☐ 6	☐ 6
☐ 7	☐ 7	☐ 7	☐ 7

Lower Boundary Notes

Upper Boundary Notes

Middle of the Staff Notes

On the Lines

In the Spaces

To the Ledger Lines

Small Intervals

Wide Intervals

Random Note-heads

Ledger Lines

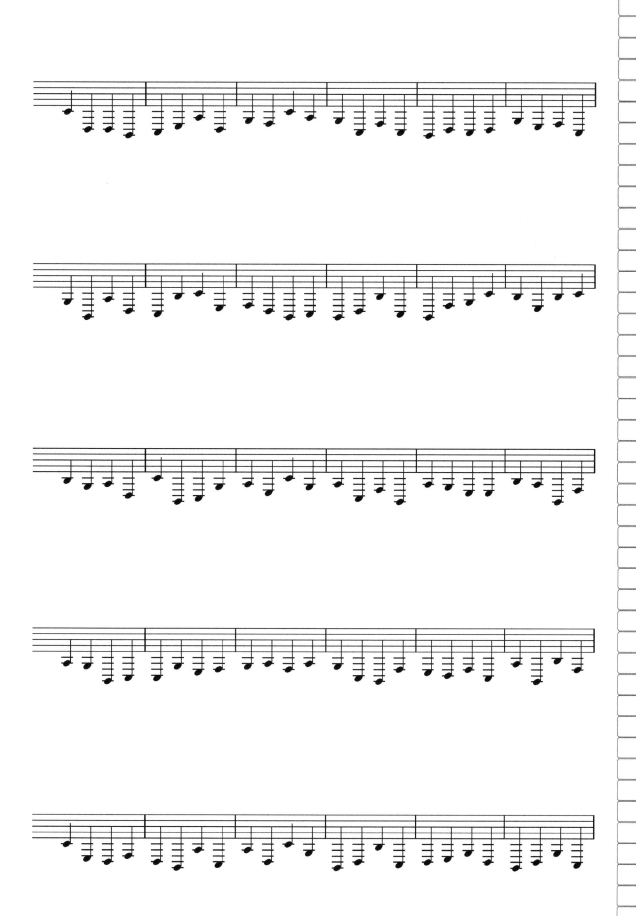

Addendum 3: Final Test

Workbook II Final Test

Student:

Sight-Reading:
Watch for key signatures and clefs.
One hand at a time. Play in a steady tempo.

Scales:
Hit the root of the scale with LH and hold it,
while you play the scale up and down two octaves with RH.
Eighth notes at ♩ = 80

Take note of the key signature.
Work out what the chords are that correlate to the roman numerals.
Construct triad voicings using appropriate inversions.
Play the progression in a slow-medium tempo motown/R&B style.
Count off the tempo as you would for a band.

I   III   vi   IV   iv   I   bVII   I

Construct chord voicings using appropriate inversions.
Play the progression in a simple slow pop/rock ballad style.
Use the sustain pedal tastefully.
Count off the tempo as you would for a band.

B♭   F/B♭   B♭⁷   E♭maj7   F♯dim7   Gmin   C⁷   F⁷⁽ˢᵘˢ⁴⁾   B♭

Sight-Reading (out of 8):
Scales (out of 4):
Roman numerals (out of 4):
Chord symbols (out of 4):

Total Score (out of 20):

Teacher comments:

Addendum 4 (For Teachers): Sample Syllabus

Weekly Lesson Plan

Week 1
In Class: Personal introductions. Discuss backgrounds and goals. Go over syllabus. Review Final Test—teacher demonstrate and briefly explain. Teacher performance.
Assignment: Get workbook. Read Introduction and complete section 1.

Week 2
Discuss Section 1. Complete Section 2. Work on sight-reading (Addendum 2).

Week 3
Complete Section 3. Discuss fundamental techniques and progressions.

Week 4
Complete Section 4. Work on minor scales (Addendum 1).

Week 5
Complete Section 5.
   Continue weekly work on scales and sight-reading for the rest of the term

Week 6
Work on Section 6.

Week 7
Complete Section 6. Composition. Complete 16-bar demo recording.

Week 8
Work on Section 7.

Week 9
Complete Section 7. Composition. Complete 16-bar demo recording.

Week 10
Work on Section 8. Choose a Jam to perform live, with the play-along track.

Week 11
Complete Section 8. Composition. Complete 16-bar demo recording.

Week 12
Complete Section 9. Record with ii–V–I play-along track.

Week 13
Work on Section 10.

Week 14
Complete Section 10. Composition. Complete 16-bar demo recording.

Week 15
Complete Section 11. Record with Blues play-along track.

Week 16
Final Test (Addendum 3).